An Analysis of

Sandra M. Gilbert and Susan Gubar's

The Madwoman in the Attic:
The Woman Writer and the Nineteenth-Century Literary Imagination

Rebecca Pohl

Published by Macat International Ltd
24:13 Coda Centre, 189 Munster Road, London SW6 6AW.

Distributed exclusively by Routledge
2 Park Square, Milton Park, Abingdon, Oxon OX14 4RN
711 Third Avenue, New York, NY 10017, USA

Routledge is an imprint of the Taylor & Francis Group, an informa business

Printed by CPI Group (UK) Ltd, Croydon CRO 4YY

www.macat.com
info@macat.com

Cataloguing in Publication Data
A catalogue record for this book is available from the British Library.
Library of Congress Cataloguing-in-Publication Data is available upon request.
Cover illustration: Capucine Deslouis

ISBN 978-1-912453-54-2 (hardback)
ISBN 978-1-912453-09-2 (paperback)
ISBN 978-1-912453-24-5 (e-book)

Notice
The information in this book is designed to orientate readers of the work under analysis,
to elucidate and contextualise its key ideas and themes, and to aid in the development
of critical thinking skills. It is not meant to be used, nor should it be used, as a
substitute for original thinking or in place of original writing or research. References and
notes are provided for informational purposes and their presence does not constitute
endorsement of the information or opinions therein. This book is presented solely for
educational purposes. It is sold on the understanding that the publisher is not engaged
to provide any scholarly advice. The publisher has made every effort to ensure that
this book is accurate and up-to-date, but makes no warranties or representations with
regard to the completeness or reliability of the information it contains. The information
and the opinions provided herein are not guaranteed or warranted to produce particular
results and may not be suitable for students of every ability. The publisher shall not be
liable for any loss, damage or disruption arising from any errors or omissions, or from
the use of this book, including, but not limited to, special, incidental, consequential or
other damages caused, or alleged to have been caused, directly or indirectly, by the
information contained within.

CONTENTS

THE MACAT LIBRARY

The Macat Library is a series of unique academic explorations of seminal works in the humanities and social sciences – books and papers that have had a significant and widely recognised impact on their disciplines. It has been created to serve as much more than just a summary of what lies between the covers of a great book. It illuminates and explores the influences on, ideas of, and impact of that book. Our goal is to offer a learning resource that encourages critical thinking and fosters a better, deeper understanding of important ideas.

Each publication is divided into three Sections: Influences, Ideas, and Impact. Each Section has four Modules. These explore every important facet of the work, and the responses to it.

This Section-Module structure makes a Macat Library book easy to use, but it has another important feature. Because each Macat book is written to the same format, it is possible (and encouraged!) to cross-reference multiple Macat books along the same lines of inquiry or research. This allows the reader to open up interesting interdisciplinary pathways.

To further aid your reading, lists of glossary terms and people mentioned are included at the end of this book (these are indicated by an asterisk [*] throughout) – as well as a list of works cited.

Macat has worked with the University of Cambridge to identify the elements of critical thinking and understand the ways in which six different skills combine to enable effective thinking.
Three allow us to fully understand a problem; three more give us the tools to solve it. Together, these six skills make up the **PACIER** model of critical thinking. They are:

ANALYSIS – understanding how an argument is built
EVALUATION – exploring the strengths and weaknesses of an argument
INTERPRETATION – understanding issues of meaning

CREATIVE THINKING – coming up with new ideas and fresh connections
PROBLEM-SOLVING – producing strong solutions
REASONING – creating strong arguments

To find out more, visit **WWW.MACAT.COM.**

CRITICAL THINKING AND *THE MADWOMAN IN THE ATTIC*

Primary critical thinking skill: INTERPRETATION
Secondary critical thinking skill: ANALYSIS

The major contribution that Sandra M. Gilbert and Susan Gubar made with *The Madwoman in the Attic* was to shift assumptions about the place of writing by women in the literary tradition. They approach this through the practice of interpretation—or, more specifically, reinterpretation. One core purpose of their work is highlighting problems of definition and questioning whether the standard interpretations of literature that have been applied hitherto are justified. As such, their book can be seen as encouraging and modelling the skill of interpretation, not just for its own sake, but as a way of recovering meaning and value in texts that would otherwise be passed over—especially writing by women and representing women.

Their focus on interpretation highlights patterns and repetitions, even a logic of patriarchal representations. *Madwoman* also encourages and models the critical skill of analysis, therefore, by looking carefully for assumptions, structures, and relationships in existing arguments about women in literature. The book's weight and significance is in its combination of conviction and commitment, together with its careful analytical method.

ABOUT THE AUTHORS OF THE ORIGINAL WORK

Sandra M. Gilbert (b. 1936) and **Susan Gubar** (b. 1944) met as young academics at the University of Indiana, where they began a lifelong academic collaboration. Their collaborative debut, *The Madwoman in the Attic* (1979), was a ground-breaking study of women's writing in a male-dominated literary field and remains an influential reference point. Gilbert and Gubar went on to publish *No Man's Land: The Place of the Woman Writer in the Twentieth Century* (1988–1994), a three-volume follow-up to their Anglo-American Victorian study. They also co-edited the field-defining *Norton Anthology of Literature by Women: The Tradition in English* (1985).

ABOUT THE AUTHOR OF THE ANALYSIS

Rebecca Pohl is the co-editor of *Rupert Thomson: Critical Essays* (2016) and has published on contemporary women's writing, gender, and feminist theory. Her work in progress includes a manuscript that examines the impact of gender on mid-century experimental writing by women in Britain. She also regularly speaks at public events on the topics of women's writing and gender, and sexuality. Pohl is Honorary Research Fellow in English Literature at the University of Manchester, Associate Lecturer at Goldsmiths University London, and a contemporary literature supervisor at the University of Cambridge.

ABOUT MACAT

GREAT WORKS FOR CRITICAL THINKING

Macat is focused on making the ideas of the world's great thinkers accessible and comprehensible to everybody, everywhere, in ways that promote the development of enhanced critical thinking skills.

It works with leading academics from the world's top universities to produce new analyses that focus on the ideas and the impact of the most influential works ever written across a wide variety of academic disciplines. Each of the works that sit at the heart of its growing library is an enduring example of great thinking. But by setting them in context – and looking at the influences that shaped their authors, as well as the responses they provoked – Macat encourages readers to look at these classics and game-changers with fresh eyes. Readers learn to think, engage and challenge their ideas, rather than simply accepting them.

'Macat offers an amazing first-of-its-kind tool for interdisciplinary learning and research. Its focus on works that transformed their disciplines and its rigorous approach, drawing on the world's leading experts and educational institutions, opens up a world-class education to anyone.'

Andreas Schleicher
Director for Education and Skills, Organisation for Economic Co-operation and Development

'Macat is taking on some of the major challenges in university education ... They have drawn together a strong team of active academics who are producing teaching materials that are novel in the breadth of their approach.'

Prof Lord Broers,
former Vice-Chancellor of the University of Cambridge

'The Macat vision is exceptionally exciting. It focuses upon new modes of learning which analyse and explain seminal texts which have profoundly influenced world thinking and so social and economic development. It promotes the kind of critical thinking which is essential for any society and economy. This is the learning of the future.'

Rt Hon Charles Clarke, former UK Secretary of State for Education

'The Macat analyses provide immediate access to the critical conversation surrounding the books that have shaped their respective discipline, which will make them an invaluable resource to all of those, students and teachers, working in the field.'

Professor William Tronzo, University of California at San Diego

WAYS IN TO THE TEXT

KEY POINTS

- Sandra M. Gilbert and Susan Gubar are two feminist*
  US-American* literary scholars who co-authored a ground-
  breaking study of writing by nineteenth-century British and
  US-American women.

- Gilbert and Gubar argue that nineteenth-century women
  writers contributed to a distinctive female literary tradition
  and poetics* predicated on the metaphor of confinement.

- Their study represents a founding moment in feminist
  literary history and theory and drew critical attention to
  women's writing.

Who Are Sandra M. Gilbert And Susan Gubar?

Sandra M. Gilbert and Susan Gubar met as young English literature academics at Indiana University and bonded over their shared minority status as New Yorkers and as women in what they describe as a "shocking[ly]" Midwestern department dominated by male scholars.[1] After team-teaching an undergraduate course on women's writing, they collaborated on writing *The Madwoman in the Attic: The Woman Writer and the Nineteenth-Century Literary Imagination* (1979), in which they drew on the conversations generated by the course, both between each other and with their students. Conversation and collaboration are key aspects of their critical approach, and they continued to collaborate over the next several decades. Further projects include the three-volume *No Man's Land: The Place of the Woman Writer in the Twentieth Century* (1988-1994) and the field-defining *Norton Anthology of Literature by Women: The Tradition in English* (1985). Gilbert and Gubar were named among *USA Today*'s "People Who Made a Difference" in 1985 and "Woman of the Year" by *Ms* magazine in 1986. In 2013, the two women were joint recipients of the National Book Critic Circle's Lifetime Achievement Award. Their popular success, coupled with their demonstrable professional success, is one of the hallmarks of their joint feminist project, which speaks to academics and general readers alike.

What Does *Madwoman* Say?

Gilbert and Gubar's extensive study of nineteenth-century women's writing in English is a project of definition. They set out to trace a distinctive female literary tradition and aesthetic,* what they refer to as "recover[ing] neglected" female literature and history,[2] specifically in the context of a male-dominated literary culture. In order to do this, they close read* key women writers from nineteenth-century British and US-American literature: Jane Austen,* Elizabeth Barrett-Browning,* Charlotte Brontë,* Emily Brontë,* Emily Dickinson,* George Eliot,* Christina Rossetti,* and Mary Shelley.* Their aim is to show how, far from working in isolation, these women writers were in dialogue with each other, across time and space, thus creating an identifiable female literary tradition.

This tradition is characterized by the metaphor of enclosure—and relatedly, escape—which Gilbert and Gubar identify as central to Victorian* women's writing. Enclosure here refers to the women writers in their social, historical, and cultural contexts as well as serving as a dominant motif in their writing. As Gilbert and Gubar contend, "Enclosed in the architecture of an overwhelmingly male-dominated society, these literary women were also, inevitably, trapped in the specifically literary constructs of what Gertrude Stein* was to call "patriarchal poetry."[3] They thus make a strong link between each author's biography and her writing, arguing that women were trapped in society, that women writers were trapped in a sexist literary tradition, and that these confinements were channelled into and challenged by the texts they wrote. The book is underpinned by the famous feminist slogan "The personal is political."*

Gilbert and Gubar see the feminist poetics they identify as operating in a transatlantic* context as well as across genres (they focus on poetry and fiction). They claim that the female tradition and poetics they identify can be applied to all nineteenth-century women's writing.

Why Does *Madwoman* Matter?

Madwoman remains a foundational book for feminist literary studies as well as for literary studies more broadly because it was one of the first studies to offer a systematic and extensive reappraisal of canonical* texts. By putting the novels and poetry they close read together under the aegis of "women's writing" rather than, for instance, "Victorian poetry" or "the nineteenth-century novel," Gilbert and Gubar are able to trace connections and continuities across women's writing that might otherwise go unnoticed. Their analysis demonstrates that women writers were not anomalous in the nineteenth century; indeed, they were very active and in conversation with each other. Gilbert and Gubar's analysis also shows that these women writers were actively rebelling—through their writing—against the social pressures they faced. These were primarily associated with the Victorian ideal of femininity, which would have women be passive and receptive rather than active and productive. Gilbert and Gubar foreground gender as a key analytical category and a key influence on literary creation.

Madwoman is now also an important historical document, recording the progress of feminist literary theory. It can be seen as one point of origin for feminist literary history: the book marks the shift in feminist literary analysis from a focus on images of women in well-known texts by men, to a focus on texts actually written by women. Although it has been heavily critiqued since its first publication in 1979, primarily for tending towards essentialist* critique, Gilbert and Gubar's study has enabled subsequent intersectional analysis* by compiling a corpus* that can be revisited and re-read. The book also models the importance of paying close attention to textual details while also situating these details—for example imagery, metaphor, and repetition—in a historical context. It was a finalist for the 1979 National Book Critics Circle Award and the 1980 Pulitzer Prize.

NOTES

1   Sandra M. Gilbert and Susan Gubar, *The Madwoman in the Attic: The Woman Writer and the Nineteenth-Century Literary Imagination*, 2nd ed. (New Haven, CT: Yale University Press, 2000), •••.

2   Gilbert and Gubar, *Madwoman,* •• ••

3   Gilbert and Gubar, *Madwoman,* ••••

SECTION 1
INFLUENCES

MODULE 1
THE AUTHOR AND THE HISTORICAL CONTEXT

KEY POINTS

- *The Madwoman in the Attic* is a foundational book in feminist literary history that continues to engender debate.
- Both Sandra M. Gilbert and Susan Gubar have had illustrious academic careers that can be described as field-defining.
- Their shared background of familial immigration and being young female academics in the early 1970s heavily influenced their intellectual collaboration and friendship.

Why Read This Text?

The Madwoman in the Attic: The Woman Writer and the Nineteenth-Century Literary Imagination is a key work of second-wave feminist* literary scholarship. It was the first academic study to trace a distinct female tradition, what Sandra M. Gilbert and Susan Gubar refer to as a "subculture,"[1] in Victorian literature. It was also one of the very first studies to gather together novels and poetry under the rubric of "women's writing," thus enabling these texts to be read through the lens of gender. This, in turn, revealed patterns of language and imagery as well as intertextual* relations that had been hitherto overlooked.

Gilbert and Gubar effectively evidence the existence of a female literary tradition, demonstrating that by the nineteenth century, women writers were far from anomalous. This disrupts conventional narratives of literary creation as predominantly male and can be considered one of the volume's main contributions to the field. The

> **❝ What did we think we were doing? Professors were people with tweed jackets, big heavy clumpy shoes, and pipes! ❞**
>
> Sandra M. Gilbert and Susan Gubar, interview in *American Vanguard*

other main contribution the book makes is the way of reading it models, which was radical at the time and can today be classed as paranoid reading.* Gilbert and Gubar approach their corpus from a psychoanalytical* perspective, uncovering female anger and rebellion beneath the customary interpretations of writing by Jane Austen, the Brontës, and Emily Dickinson, among others.

The book also represents a key example of feminist methodology with its insistence on intellectual collaboration and the connections it draws between the personal and the political.

The importance of *Madwoman* is tied to its time of publication, 1979. While its central arguments may appear self-evident to the present-day reader, it is important to remember that the inclusion of women writers in literary history and the canon* as well as the systematic critical analysis of gender are recent developments. Though often considered very much "of its time," *Madwoman* continues to generate debate today as evidenced by a 2009 collection of essays marking its thirtieth anniversary: *Gilbert and Gubar's* The Madwoman in the Attic *After Thirty Years*. In her review of this volume, Elaine Showalter* names *Madwoman* "one of the three most transformative works of US-American literary criticism of the late twentieth century," placing it alongside Edward Said's* *Orientalism* (1978) and Eve Kosofsky Sedgwick's* *Between Men* (1985).[2]

Authors' Lives

Sandra M. Gilbert, Professor Emerita of English at the University of California (UC), Davis is an US-American feminist* literary scholar and acclaimed poet. Educated at Cornell University (BA, 1957), Gilbert received her PhD from Columbia University with a specialization in twentieth-century poetry, bringing together Modernism* and Romanticism.* She joined the faculty of UC Davis in 1975. Gilbert has also taught at Indiana, Johns Hopkins, Princeton, and Stanford universities as well as at California State, Hayward, and Williams colleges. She was the inaugural M. H. Abrams Distinguished Visiting Professor at Cornell University in 2007.

In 1996, Gilbert served as president of the largest professional body for literary scholars, the Modern Languages Association. She has received multiple major fellowships and published widely in the field of literary studies. Her monographs include *Acts of Attention: The Poems of D.H. Lawrence* (1972) and *Rereading Women: Thirty Years of Exploring Our Literary Traditions* (2011). In addition to her scholarly work, she has authored eight collections of poetry, receiving the Patterson Prize for *Ghost Volcano* (1997) and an American Book Award for *Kissing the Bread: New and Selected Poems 1969-1999* (2000).

Susan Gubar, Professor Emerita of English and Women's Studies at Indiana University, is a US-American feminist literary scholar and writer. She was educated at The City College of New York (BA, 1965) and the University of Michigan (MA, 1968). In 1972, she received her PhD from the University of Iowa with a specialization in the eighteenth-century novel and joined Indiana University's faculty in 1973.

Gubar has been the recipient of numerous awards. She has published widely on literature and gender and more recently on race and religion. Titles include *Racechanges* (1997) and *Judas: A Biography* (2009). Chronicling her experience of ovarian cancer, Gubar is now a columnist for the *New York Times* online ("Living with Cancer") and has written a memoir, *Memoir of a Debulked Woman* (2012).

Authors' Backgrounds
Both Gilbert and Gubar are the children of immigrants: Gilbert's

father's family emigrated from Paris and her mother's family from Sicily, while Gubar is of German-Jewish descent. Gilbert has suggested that their shared interest in the "palimpsestic subplots of women's texts" might be traced back to their family histories,[3] which are characterised by the gaps and omissions caused by emigration.

Gilbert, who began writing poetry at the age of four, considers herself primarily a poet, acknowledging in an interview that her "deepest identity always was as a poet."[4] Nevertheless, she pursued graduate work in literature, examining D. H. Lawrence's* poetry.

When they met in the elevator at Indiana University's Ballantine Hall in 1973, Gilbert and Gubar were two young mothers and young academics as well as native New Yorkers—indeed, they have both retained their strong Brooklyn accents as identity markers throughout decades of teaching and researching on the West Coast and in the Midwest, respectively. Feeling afloat in the Midwest, they quickly formed a strong intellectual and personal attachment to one another.

Despite now being identified as feminist trailblazers, neither Gilbert nor Gubar identified as feminists when they first met at Indiana. Neither their training nor their research was especially woman-focused when they began working on *The Madwoman in the Attic*.

NOTES

1   Sandra M. Gilbert and Susan Gubar, *The Madwoman in the Attic: The Woman Writer and the Nineteenth-Century Literary Imagination*, 2nd ed. (New Haven, CT: Yale University Press, 2000), ⋯-, passim.

2   Elaine Showalter, "Gilbert & Gubar's *The Madwoman in the Attic* After Thirty Years," *Victorian Studies* 53.4 (2011): 715.

3   Gilbert and Gubar, *Madwoman*, ⋯. See also Marysa Demoor and Katrien Heene, "State of the Art: Of Influences and Anxieties, Sandra Gilbert's Feminist Commitment," *The European Journal of Women's Studies* 9.2 (2002): 181-98.

4   Jacqueline Vaught Brogan, "Interview with Sandra M. Gilbert," *Women's Studies* 38.4 (2009): 400.

MODULE 2
ACADEMIC CONTEXT

KEY POINTS

- *The Madwoman in the Attic* made a case for the importance of context—biographical, historical, social— to the study of literature.
- Gilbert and Gubar were in the vanguard of US-American feminist literary studies, which included works by Ellen Moers,* Elaine Showalter, and Kate Millet.*
- Harold Bloom's* influential concept of "the anxiety of influence" was adapted by Gilbert and Gubar as "the anxiety of authorship."

The Work In Its Context

At the time when Sandra M. Gilbert and Susan Gubar met as young academics, Anglo-American literary criticism was dominated by the school of New Criticism,* a formalist* approach to literature developed primarily by I.A. Richards* and William Empson* that treated literary texts as autonomous. New Critics located meaning in a text irrespective of any context (biographical, historical, literary). They argued that it doesn't matter who wrote a text or where or when; its literary value as well as its meaning can be derived purely from analyzing its form and structure. This approach to literary analysis, which had become influential after World War I, was increasingly challenged in the 1970s as the political and social critiques of the 1960s gained momentum and university literature programs explored the inequalities that the women's liberation movement and others (for example, anti-racist and anti-homophobic movements) had sought to expose and challenge.

> **“** *Madwoman* introduced a revolutionary way of reading
> and radically expanded the textual field of nineteenth-
> and twentieth-century literature for students and
> scholars.[3] **”**
>
> Elaine Showalter, *Gilbert & Gubar's* The Madwoman in the Attic *After Thirty Years*

While both Gilbert and Gubar have said that they did not come to the project that evolved into *The Madwoman in the Attic: The Woman Writer and the Nineteenth-Century Literary Imagination* as feminists—indeed, the module that provided the germ for the book was proposed by their department chair at the time—Gubar has also stressed the importance of the women's movement as a context for their encounter with each other and with the texts they subsequently analyzed. The fact that their pioneering study originated in the classroom is an important aspect of the project's feminist methodology and one that both Gilbert and Gubar emphasize when they discuss their work. Gilbert has called the experience "electrifying," and Gubar has described the seminar as "an extraordinary intellectual adventure that was deeply pedagogic. We really did learn by creating lesson plans, by chatting with our students."[1] In this sense, the seminar and the subsequent book are examples and results of the second-wave feminist practice of consciousness-raising and the politicizing of scholarly endeavors.

The corpus must also be seen in this context. As Gilbert describes it, the two academics simply compiled a list of books by women they knew of and then expanded it with texts they encountered in that process (e.g. by Kate Chopin* and Charlotte Perkins Gilman*).

Overview Of The Field
When Gilbert and Gubar convened their seminar on nineteenth-century women's writing in 1974, they had no strong precedents or

role models to guide them. By the time they published their insights in the shape of a book in 1979, only a handful of other feminist studies focused on women's writing had been or were being published. These included Patricia Meyers Spacks'* *The Female Imagination* (1975), Elaine Showalter's *A Literature of Their Own* (1977), and Ellen Moers' *Literary Women* (1976). In this sense, there was hardly a tradition, literary or scholarly, to write into—Gilbert and Gubar had to create their own, essentially helping create the field of women's writing and feminist literary history. As Gilbert puts it in the introduction to the second edition of their book (2000), their research was partly driven by their "feelings of elation about being present at an originatory moment."[2]

Early feminist criticism in literature was predominantly concerned with critiquing the representation of women. Another key text from the period is Kate Millet's influential *Sexual Politics* (1970), which interrogated the representation of women in canonical texts by male writers such as D. H. Lawrence, Norman Mailer,* and Henry Miller.* Millet showed the misogyny* inherent in all these writers' texts when it came to their representation of women and gender relations. Gilbert and Gubar expanded this analysis beyond the representation or images of women by including writing *by*, not just *about*, women, adding a crucial dimension to the emerging field of feminist literary analysis.

Academic Influences

Although the field was only just being established, Gilbert and Gubar do credit a number of feminist scholars in their introduction, especially feminist historians such as Gerda Lerner,* Alice Rossi,* Ann Douglas,* Martha Vicinus,* Carroll Smith-Rosenberg,* and Nancy Cott.* It is significant that the earliest feminist criticism can be found in analyses of history, making its way into analyses of literature only as scholars abandoned the New Critics' quarantining of the literary text from its contexts. Gilbert and Gubar also explicitly credit Showalter and Moers, whose books compiled a longer historical narrative of women's writing. This allowed Gilbert and Gubar to focus on one specific period, and they chose the nineteenth century.

Perhaps the most formative conceptual influence on *Madwoman* is the work of Harold Bloom, and by extension that of Sigmund Freud.* In his famous study *The Anxiety of Influence* (1973), Bloom adopts Freud's notion of the Oedipus complex* to explain the development of the Western literary tradition. He argues that authors—of which his examples are overwhelmingly male—suffer from what he calls the "anxiety of influence." This anxiety refers to a writer's fear of being overshadowed by his or her literary predecessors—that is, fear that the writer's work will remain merely derivative rather than being an original creation. This leads to an agonistic (conflict-driven) model of literary creation, whereby the son (the writer) must slay the father (earlier writers) in order to create. Bloom posits a number of methods writers may use to achieve this symbolic death of the father, all of which are forms of "creative misprision" or deliberate misreading of influential texts, which then allow the younger writer to stake a claim for his or her own creativity. It is this idea of "the anxiety of influence" that Gilbert and Gubar adapt in their analysis of women's writing, now calling it "the anxiety of authorship."

NOTES

1   Sandra Gilbert and Susan Gubar, interview by Eli Nadeau, *American Vanguard,* January 21, 2013, http://nbcc.americanvanguardpress.com/balakian-sandrof-awards/gg.html.

2   Sandra M. Gilbert and Susan Gubar, *The Madwoman in the Attic: The Woman Writer and the Nineteenth-Century Literary Imagination*, 2nd ed. (New Haven, CT: Yale University Press, 2000), ···.

MODULE 3
THE PROBLEM

KEY POINTS

- *The Madwoman in the Attic* asks what might characterize a women's literary tradition.

- One of the distinctive features of *Madwoman* is its indebtedness to conversation, especially in and around the classroom.

- *Madwoman* helped initiate a debate around women's writing rather than intervening in an established discussion.

Core Question

The women's liberation movement was interrogating the role gender played in society and proposing a radical politics of change at the time when Sandra M. Gilbert and Susan Gubar met and embarked on their collaboration. As Gilbert has since put it, "the Second Wave of the women's movement was about to crest."[1] So the question of gender was part of much of contemporary culture, including increasingly within literary studies. However, the work that had been done towards challenging gender inequality in literature, most notably Kate Millet's study on sexual politics, relied on an analysis of texts by men. This approach, "Images of Women" criticism, thus inadvertently perpetuated the marginalization of women it intended to critique. Feminist critics were now looking to develop a more woman-centered approach to literary analysis.

Gilbert and Gubar intervened at this point. Their insistence on reading women writers only and together responded to doubts about the existence and quality of a women's literary tradition. Taking issue

> **"** Much like any other radical critic, the feminist critic can be seen as the product of a struggle mainly concerned with social and political change; her specific role within it becomes an attempt to extend such general political action to the cultural domain. **"**
>
> Toril Moi, *Sexual/Textual Politics*

with the dominant metaphor of literary paternity, which occludes and excludes women's creative practice from the canon and from literary history, Gilbert and Gubar investigate nineteenth-century women's writing in an effort to determine patterns that constitute a distinctively female creative practice and tradition—a feminist poetics of rebellion.

The Participants

By the time Gilbert and Gubar met, the women's movement was well underway, though it had yet to make a discernible impact in university literature departments. While not explicitly concerned with literature, important precursor publications that outlined gender inequality and called for radical change included Betty Friedan's* *The Feminine Mystique* (1963), Germaine Greer's* *The Female Eunuch* (1970), and Shulamith Firestone's* *The Dialectic of Sex* (1970).

Within literary studies, Elaine Showalter pursued a similar line of investigation to that of Gilbert and Gubar, though she focused exclusively on the British novel by women in the nineteenth century. Her major conceptual contribution to the field is the notion of gynocriticism,* which aims to identify a distinct female canon, autonomous of the male tradition, in which women explore their distinctive—but socially and historically situated—experience.

Gilbert and Gubar stress, in the introduction to their book as much as in subsequent interviews and statements, how important the space of the classroom was to the formation of their critical project. The students who attended their seminar in 1974 are thus positioned as key participants in the discussions that generated *The Madwoman in the Attic: The Woman Writer and the Nineteenth-Century Literary Imagination.* As a collaborative project, the book stands out amongst academic texts and further highlights the importance of community to Gilbert and Gubar's work. *Madwoman* came into being through conversation and collaboration, which was also the source of the "exhilaration" that marked their writing.[2]

The Contemporary Debate

During the time that Gilbert and Gubar were working on *Madwoman*, the debate amongst British and US-American literary scholars regarding women's writing was only just emerging. There was not even a widespread awareness of the absence of such a debate. The general assumption, implicit in contemporary publications, conferences, and syllabi, maintained that there was little to no significant literary output by women. There was, however, an emerging debate about women's equality that took the shape of the women's liberation movement, or what we now often refer to as second-wave feminism. For Gubar, though, this debate was "'only accessed […] through the intellectual journey of the collaboration" with Gilbert.[3] Gilbert and Gubar shared Showalter's project of delineating a female literary tradition and explicitly built on her work (which they accessed in its doctoral form at UC Davis), though they are less careful about making universalizing claims about female creativity.

Feminist literary critics were part of the formation of a larger field of women's writing. The recovery work they all engaged in depended on the books, poems, diaries, and letters of the writers in question being made available. This task was taken on by a growing number of feminist publishing houses, most significantly The Feminist Press in New York and Virago in London. It was only due to the Feminist

Press's republication of Charlotte Perkins Gilman's *The Yellow Wallpaper* in 1973 that the text was available for Gilbert and Gubar to teach and then write about.

NOTES

1   Jacqueline Vaught Brogan, "Interview with Sandra M. Gilbert," *Women's Studies* 38.4 (2009): 405.

2   Sandra M. Gilbert and Susan Gubar, *The Madwoman in the Attic: The Woman Writer and the Nineteenth-Century Literary Imagination*, 2nd ed. (New Haven, CT: Yale University Press, 2000), ·–.

3   Sandra Gilbert and Susan Gubar, interview by Eli Nadeau, *American Vanguard,* January 21, 2013, http://nbcc.americanvanguardpress.com/balakian–sandrof-awards/gg.html.

MODULE 4
THE AUTHOR'S CONTRIBUTION

KEY POINTS

- The aim of *The Madwoman in the Attic* is to trace a women's literary tradition and poetics through an analysis of nineteenth-century writing by women.

- Gilbert and Gubar used a series of extended close readings that were situated in their social and cultural contexts to achieve that goal.

- Their work made an identifiable corpus of Victorian women's writing available and demonstrated the importance of gender as a category for literary analysis.

Authors' Aims

The Madwoman in the Attic: The Woman Writer and the Nineteenth-Century Literary Imagination is primarily a work of literary history in which Sandra M. Gilbert and Susan Gubar attempt to show that "women's past is not always quite the same as men's."[1] However, it is just as much a work of literary scholarship in its endeavour to unearth a feminist poetics, which Gilbert and Gubar describe as "a common, female impulse to struggle free from social and literary confinement through strategic redefinitions of self, art, and society."[2] Their aim, and their original contribution to scholarship, is to identify the characteristics of female literary production within a patriarchal literary system. In this way, they challenged orthodox literary history, which pushed women writers to the margins of literary creativity, explaining them away as anomalies and oddities. Instead, Gilbert and Gubar aimed to uncover the many connections and parallels between what looked like disparate moments of female literary creativity in, for example,

> **❝** Susan and I are not prophets, we are cultural, literary and psychoanalytic historians. **❞**
>
> Marysa Demoor and Katrien Heene, "State of the Art: Of Influences and Anxieties, Sandra Gilbert's Feminist Commitment"

Charlotte Brontë and Emily Dickinson. Building on earlier feminist analyses of representations of women in literature, Gilbert and Gubar set out to propose a firmly woman-centered approach that focused on the presence of women writers rather than their absence.

Approach

Building on the work of Elaine Showalter and Ellen Moers, *Madwoman* gathers together literary texts from the United Kingdom and the United States written by women across the nineteenth century. Gilbert and Gubar offer extended close readings of selected novels and poetry by mostly canonical writers such as Jane Austen, Charlotte Brontë, and Emily Dickinson. Nevertheless, their analysis is resolutely contextual, which means it does not treat its objects (the novels and poems) as autonomous, but rather sees them as representative and expressive of socio-historical and especially psychological conditions.

For Gilbert and Gubar (and many other feminist scholars at the time), this meant adopting a biographical approach, linking the biographies of the authors with the characters they have written. They are, in other words, interested in the images of women created by women. Literary creation is seen as expressive of the writer and her biographical, social, and historical context.

Such a biographical approach, though it may seem outdated now, can also be seen as feminist in as much as it reflects the slogan "The personal is political."[3] Gilbert and Gubar have remarked that their reading of women writers and the ensuing insights into literary production coincided with their own feminist awakening: "we have inevitably ended up reading our own lives as well as the texts we study."[4] It is in this context, too, that the choice of period for their analysis, the nineteenth century, should be seen. Romanticism and its legacies are significant to Gilbert and Gubar because of what they call the "Romantic heritage of aesthetic and political rebellion."[5] It is amid the tensions between emancipatory political activism and powerful ideologies of femininity such as the ideal wife or "Angel in the House"* that Gilbert and Gubar locate feminist criticism's "vital origins."[6]

Just as importantly, Gilbert and Gubar focus on the nineteenth century because it is during this period that they make out a critical mass of women writers, what they refer to as "an unprecedentedly powerful and startlingly empowering sisterhood."[7]

Alongside the contextual, psychoanalytical* approach, Gilbert and Gubar's analysis stands out for its focus on metaphors. One crucial aspect of their approach and indeed their contribution is their critical engagement with the conventional metaphors of literary production. They show how these are gendered in particular ways and are inherently patriarchal.* They then offer alternative images and metaphors through which to think about literary production.

Contribution In Context

Gilbert and Gubar's book contributed to making the absence of women's writing from critical discourse visible and to kick-starting a debate around it. Together with Moers and Showalter, they demonstrated the contribution women writers had made to modern literature, though crucially they did this from a feminist perspective that focused on women's writing and the specific characteristics that marked this writing. This involved claiming gender as a meaningful category for literary analysis, making explicit assumptions surrounding gender and creativity, tracing a tradition of women's writing, and contributing to a mode of reading literary texts that accounts for contexts of various kinds. *Madwoman* also argues for the importance of reading between the lines of a text, of discovering what is left unsaid or what is even concealed.

Madwoman is also an important step in the development of twentieth-century literary criticism. At the time when Gilbert and Gubar wrote their book, Modernism had come to seem like a dominant and largely masculine literary tradition that valued text-centered critical approaches such as the formalist New Criticism. Context-centered approaches like the one proposed by Gilbert and Gubar challenged the aesthetic autonomy of texts by asking questions about the circumstances in which they were written and then read to draw out inequalities, for instance in terms of gender and race representation.

NOTES

1   Sandra M. Gilbert and Susan Gubar, *The Madwoman in the Attic: The Woman Writer and the Nineteenth-Century Literary Imagination*, 2nd ed. (New Haven, CT: Yale University Press, 2000), •••

2   Gilbert and Gubar, *Madwoman*, •

••   Carol Hanisch, "The Personal is Political," *The Personal to Political: The Women's Liberation Movement Classic With a New Explanatory Introduction*, February 1969, www.carolhanish.org/CHwritings/PIP.html.

4   Gilbert and Gubar, *Madwoman*, •.

5   Gilbert and Gubar, *Madwoman*, •••.

6   Gilbert and Gubar, *Madwoman*, ••

••   Gilbert and Gubar, *Madwoman*, •••

SECTION 2
IDEAS

MODULE 5
MAIN IDEAS

KEY POINTS

- Gilbert and Gubar show how the metaphor of literary paternity has determined modern Western literary production.

- They argue that the female literary tradition, as it emerges in the nineteenth century, is characterised by narratives of imprisonment and escape.

- *The Madwoman in the Attic* is written in a distinct style that is marked by its rich lyricism and is purposefully jargon-free..

Key Ideas

If the defining metaphor of Western literary creation is that of the phallic* pen, and the Western literary tradition is best conceived of as an Oedipal struggle between father and son, Sandra M. Gilbert and Susan Gubar ask, where does that leave women writers? Their response to this question is two-fold and developed in the first part of *The Madwoman in the Attic: The Woman Writer and the Nineteenth-Century Literary Imagination*, "Toward a Feminist Poetics." They begin by discussing what they call the metaphor of literary paternity coupled with a critique of male images of women, showing how male-authored texts have confined women to "the paradigmatic polarities of angel and monster,"[1] where the only way to survive is to acquiesce to passivity. They then introduce their influential idea of "the anxiety of authorship," which is women's "inevitable" response to these patriarchal representations, as creation implies action. It is the negotiation of this "anxiety of authorship," they argue, that marks the

> ❝ For the great women writers of the past two centuries are linked by the ingenuity with which all, while no one was really looking, danced out of the debilitating looking glass of the male text into the health of female authority. ❞
>
> Sandra M. Gilbert and Susan Gubar, *The Madwoman in the Attic*

Anglo-American female literary subculture of the nineteenth century. It elucidates "the dynamics of female literary response to male literary assertion and coercion."[2] This response, Gilbert and Gubar contend, is one of subversion. By tracing this rebellious response, a female literary tradition and poetics—"a sisterhood"[3]—become visible.

Exploring The Ideas

Gilbert and Gubar track the prevalence of metaphors of paternity in historical and contemporary discourses of artistic, and especially literary, creation, remarking on "our culture's historical confusion of literary authorship with patriarchal authority."[4] An important aspect of their overall argument is the close tie Gilbert and Gubar outline between representations or images of women in fictional and poetic texts (characters) and historical women as they exist in the world (persons). According to Gilbert and Gubar, women encounter the same constraints in the world as they do in texts, facing "the coercive power not only of cultural constraints but of the literary texts which incarnate them."[5] Following this logic, texts both reflect and influence culture, creating a vicious cycle whereby—in a patriarchal society— men write women as they would have them (passive, derivative), and then women have only these male-authored representations available as models for their own existence and, crucially, writing practice. The metaphor Gilbert and Gubar employ to describe this mechanism is imprisonment, arguing that women must "escape" patriarchal texts in order to achieve the artistic autonomy that will allow them to write alternatives to the dominant male-authored images of women: the angel and the monster.[6]

Literary production reflects and embodies cultural power relations, and its status quo is hence fiercely guarded by those in power. In the context of *Madwoman*, power is located with the patriarchy. Nevertheless, despite literary history's structural sexism, nineteenth-century Anglo-American women did produce literary texts.

Gilbert and Gubar set out to demonstrate that there is a tradition of women writers, constituting a female literary subculture, who found ways of overcoming patriarchal coercion and truthfully expressing female experience in texts that were successful in the wider literary field. They achieved this by creating "submerged meanings"[7] and producing "literary works that are in some sense palimpsestic, works whose surface designs conceal or obscure deeper, less accessible (and less socially acceptable) levels of meaning. Thus these authors managed the difficult task of achieving true female literary authority by simultaneously conforming to and subverting patriarchal literary standards."[8]

This notion of concealment, a plot within a plot, rebellion within conformity, is central to Gilbert and Gubar's reading of Victorian women's writing. One of the methods of writing subversion is by projecting their own anger and despair into fictional characters. Notably, these are never the heroines but usually "mad or monstrous women" such as Bertha Mason in *Jane Eyre,*[9] who inspired Gilbert and Gubar's title. These women are punished over the course of the novel or poem—Bertha burns to death—which Gilbert and Gubar take to suggest that rather than operating as a foil to the heroine, they are the author's double, "an image of her own anxiety and rage" that allows women writers to "come to terms with their own uniquely female feelings of fragmentation, their own keen sense of the discrepancies between what they are and what they are supposed to be."[10]

These subversively submerged plots and figures of rebellion rely on the imagery of entrapment and, relatedly, escape, which is of key importance to the women's writing under consideration. Locked into texts and domestic spaces, confined both figuratively and literally, women writers enacted their "claustrophobic rage"[11] by obsessively writing narratives of imprisonment and flight—so much so that these narratives, in Gilbert and Gubar's reading, characterize the female literary tradition of the nineteenth century. That this tradition, or subculture, is made visible is the primary objective of Gilbert and Gubar's analysis and is the effect of recognizing these female writing strategies: Where the crucial female image is that of the madwoman, the crucial plot is that of escape, and taken together they articulate the rebellious frustration of the woman writer in a patriarchal society. Moreover, crucially, by tracing these figures, plots, and images, a tradition of women's writing is made visible.

Language And Expression

Elaine Showalter, in her review of the anniversary collection, remarks on the "rich, dense, and unmistakable prose style of Gilbert and Gubar" and how their "stylistic innovations have been liberating and stimulating models" for feminist criticism.[12] She includes amongst these innovations the series of epigraphs that preface each chapter of *Madwoman* as well as the prevalence of alliteration, catch-phrases, lists, and parallelisms. Gilbert and Gubar are close readers, and their attention to language is crucial to their analysis. Many of their set-piece readings begin to look like deconstructionist* critiques, with their disassembling of evident and singular meaning, looking instead at hidden meanings and ambiguity. For example:

"As a creation "penned" by man, moreover, woman has been "penned up" or "penned in." As a sort of "sentence" man has spoken, she herself been "sentenced": fated, jailed, for he has both "indited" her and "indicted" her. As a thought he has "framed," she has been both "framed" (enclosed) in his texts, glyphs, graphics, and "framed up" (found guilty, found wanting) in his cosmologies."[13]

Gilbert and Gubar are reiterating a key point of their discussion here—the fact that women have been imprisoned by men in both literary and cultural narratives—purely by listing a series of double-edged terms.

The book is also jargon-free and generally considered to have been written in an accessible style, making its critical feminist analysis available to a popular readership as well as a specialist one.

NOTES

1   Sandra M. Gilbert and Susan Gubar, *The Madwoman in the Attic: The Woman Writer and the Nineteenth-Century Literary Imagination*, 2nd ed. (New Haven, CT: Yale University Press, 2000), 76.

2   Gilbert and Gubar, *Madwoman*, ·-•

3   Gilbert and Gubar, *Madwoman*, ····•

4   Gilbert and Gubar, *Madwoman*, 11.

5   Gilbert and Gubar, *Madwoman*, 11.

6   Gilbert and Gubar, *Madwoman*, 13.

7   Gilbert and Gubar, *Madwoman*, 72.

8   Gilbert and Gubar, *Madwoman*, 73.

9   Gilbert and Gubar, *Madwoman*, 78.

10 Gilbert and Gubar, *Madwoman*, 78.

11 Gilbert and Gubar, *Madwoman*, 85.

12 Elaine Showalter, "Gilbert & Gubar's *The Madwoman in the Attic* After Thirty Years," *Victorian Studies* 53.4 (2011): 716.

13 Gilbert and Gubar, *Madwoman*, 13.

MODULE 6
SECONDARY IDEAS

KEY POINTS

* *The Madwoman in the Attic* argues that the figure of
  the madwoman expresses submerged female anger in
  Victorian women's writing.

* Gilbert and Gubar provide extensive case studies to bolster
  their argument and in so doing simultaneously expand the
  Western literary canon.

* One of *Madwoman*'s most important contributions to the
  field is its modelling of feminist practice, which has been
  overlooked.

Other Themes

The "anxiety of authorship" identified by Sandra M. Gilbert and Susan
Gubar—that is, the woman writer's conflicting desire for autonomous
creation and her fear of monstrosity—led, in their reading, to anger.
This anger, socially inacceptable as it was, was not fully repressed, but
"submerged" and becomes visible in Victorian women's writing
through attention to metaphors of imprisonment and escape, illness,
and perhaps most famously the figure of the madwoman.

Alongside the overarching argument about women's writing,
Gilbert and Gubar also propose distinct readings of individual writers
in the shape of case studies. Their contribution to the reception of
each of these writers has been just as influential as their contribution
to the reception of women's writing as a whole. In particular, the
readings of Jane Austen and Charlotte Brontë advanced by *The
Madwoman in the Attic: The Woman Writer and the Nineteenth-Century
Literary Imagination* changed the way these writers were positioned

> ❝ This figure [of the madwoman] arises like a bad dream, bloody, envious, enraged as if the very process of writing had itself liberated a madwoman, a crazy and angry woman, from a silence in which neither she nor her author can continue to acquiesce. ❞
>
> Sandra M. Gilbert and Susan Gubar, *The Madwoman in the Attic*

within the literary tradition. Other writers, for example Elizabeth Barrett Browning, were only put on the map as significant contributors to a tradition by Gilbert and Gubar's revisionary work. *Madwoman* thus charts both a genealogy of women writers and intervenes in individual writers' reputations. It is this upsetting of the canon that some see as *Madwoman*'s most incisive intervention across English and US-American literature.[1]

Exploring The Ideas

Faced with the "vexed and vexing polarities of angel and monster" offered in the Victorian literary tradition,[2] how did women writers writing women characters respond? Through the use of images of anger, say Gilbert and Gubar, and the "phenomena of evasion and concealment"[3] that mark women's writing from the period and "submerge" these images. By paying close attention to metaphors and doubles, the female anger effected by a patriarchal culture becomes available in the apparently docile novels and poems written by women.

In the most famous passage from *Madwoman*, Gilbert and Gubar develop these ideas through a re-reading of Charlotte Brontë's *Jane Eyre*, in particular the figure of Rochester's first wife, Bertha Mason, who is imprisoned in the attic of Thornfield Manor. In this revisionary reading, Bertha and Jane are not rivals for Rochester's affection, nor is Bertha a warning representing failed femininity;

rather, Bertha is Jane's dark double, and theirs is the "central confrontation" in the novel.[4] Gilbert and Gubar argue that the novel is shocking because of Jane's "refusal to accept the forms, customs, and standards of society—in short, its rebellious feminism."[5] This feminist rage, however, is enacted by Bertha, whose "appearances [have] been associated with an experience (or repression) of anger on Jane's part" and who, when she finally escapes her attic prison, burns Thornfield, the symbol of Rochester's patriarchal mastery, to the ground.[6]

Through this reading of Bertha, the figure of the madwoman, maligned by male writers as one variant of the monster, is reconfigured. She is seen as a projection of Jane's, and indeed Brontë's, unutterable frustrations and desires. The madwoman is the "composite paradigm" of the angel and the monster,[7] where the monster woman "is simply a woman who seeks the power of self-articulation."[8] In the words of Gilbert and Gubar: "For it is, after all, through the violence of the double that the female author enacts her own raging desire to escape male houses and male texts, while at the same time it is through the double's violence that this anxious author articulates for herself the costly destructiveness of anger repressed until it can no longer be contained."[9] In this context, Bertha's final act is seen as a "covert expression of feminist rage."[10]

Overlooked

One aspect of Gilbert and Gubar's monumental literary study that historically has been overlooked is what Marlene Tromp* has called its "utopian vision for feminist practice."[11] Emphasizing the importance of grass-roots feminist activism at the time of *Madwoman*'s production, she argues that "The content of *Madwoman* was radical, to be sure, but so were the feminist practices that it called for and nurtured."[12] This was particularly the case in the academic context where it began, though one of the book's key achievements is precisely the bridging of activism and theory, of political agency and scholarship—a "call for community."[13] One of the venues for modelling this practice and community was the classroom, another collaborative intellectual enterprise. The valuing of pedagogy, the explicit acknowledgement of the reciprocal relationship between teaching and research, rather than the received hierarchy of male creative process (research) over female practices of care (teaching), was new—and remains unusual to this day. Similarly unusual is the collaborative nature of the publication, particularly in the humanities. *Madwoman* models a form of solidarity

NOTES

1   Susan Fraiman, "After Gilbert and Gubar: Madwomen Inspired by *Madwoman*," in *Gilbert and Gubar's* The Madwoman in the Attic *after Thirty Years*, ed. by Annette R. Federico (Columbia: University of Missouri Press, 2009), 28.

2   Sandra M. Gilbert and Susan Gubar, *The Madwoman in the Attic: The Woman Writer and the Nineteenth-Century Literary Imagination*, 2nd ed. (New Haven, CT: Yale University Press, 2000), 46.

3   Gilbert and Gubar, *Madwoman*, 75.

4   Gilbert and Gubar, *Madwoman*, 339.

5   Gilbert and Gubar, *Madwoman*, 338.

6   Gilbert and Gubar, *Madwoman*, 360.

7   Nina Auerbach, "Review of *The Madwoman in the Attic*," *Victorian Studies* 23.4 (1980): 505.

8   Gilbert and Gubar, *Madwoman*, 79.

9   Gilbert and Gubar, *Madwoman*, 85.

10 Fraiman, "After Gilbert and Gubar," 29.

11 Marlene Tromp, "Modeling the *Madwoman*: Feminist Movements and the Academy," in *Gilbert and Gubar's* The Madwoman in the Attic *after Thirty Years*, ed. by Annette R. Federico (Columbia: University of Missouri Press, 2009), 34.

12 Tromp, "Modeling the *Madwoman*," 37.

13 Tromp, "Modeling the *Madwoman*," 45.

MODULE 7
ACHIEVEMENT

KEY POINTS

- *The Madwoman in the Attic* succeeds in tracing a distinctive female literary tradition and poetics.
- The book was immediately widely read across academic and activist audiences.
- While *Madwoman*'s neglect of race and class differences is problematic, its achievement as a foundational text in literary feminism remains noteworthy.

Assessing The Argument

Sandra M. Gilbert and Susan Gubar succeeded in fulfilling their intention to showcase a female literary tradition in nineteenth-century England and the United States that contradicted conventional narratives of the successful woman writer as an anomaly in literary history. They effectively traced a distinctive female literary tradition in the nineteenth century, showing how women writers responded to and developed each other's work, albeit in often concealed or "submerged" ways. By drawing on writers across genres (poetry and fiction) and by making transatlantic connections that privilege gender as a category of analysis rather than nation, Gilbert and Gubar show that it matters what objects we choose to study. The wealth of material they gather together and present in what is an extensive literary study provide a persuasive body of evidence for their propositions.

The Madwoman in the Attic: The Woman Writer and the Nineteenth-Century Literary Imagination foregrounds the importance of context to literary analysis, and it shows the radical implications of selecting

> ❝ Gilbert and Gubar became the moguls of feminist criticism. ❞
>
> Elaine Showalter, "Gilbert & Gubar's *The Madwoman in the Attic* After Thirty Years"

which objects to analyze. In this case, the selection of only women writers, coupled with the consideration of the impact of gender on the writing and reading of Anglo-American literary texts in the nineteenth century, uncovers a previously invisible literary tradition. Gilbert and Gubar's extensive close readings of Victorian women writers and the particularities of their writing in opposition to dominant canonical texts models an inclusive critical practice that remains crucial to projects of justice and equality today. One recent example of this is the 2017 campaign to decolonize the curriculum at the University of Cambridge.

Achievement In Context

The women's liberation movement and emerging academic debates about literary feminism contributed to *Madwoman*'s success, affording a ready readership both within and beyond academics. As the first study of its kind, Gilbert and Gubar's book provided a framework for these emerging conversations and was widely read and referenced. It offered a language and a mode of reading (close, contextualized), it enacted a feminist critique within academia, and it intervened in the canon by making neglected texts by women writers visible, thus beginning to re-write Western literary history.

Its sales potential was immediately recognized by publishers, and Gilbert and Gubar received five offers of publication. By choosing to publish with Yale University Press, they ensured that their text would both be read by diverse audiences and have institutional approval. Its appearance on the general non-fiction shortlists of both the National

Book Critics Circle Award in Literature (1979) and the Pulitzer Prize (1980) further demonstrate the book's wide appeal and political import, as well as increasing its sales. At the time of publication, and in the United States in particular, *Madwoman* spoke to growing body of feminist scholars and helped shape the emerging debates around women's literary criticism and history as a reflection of the wider political activism of the day.

Limitations

Madwoman has been heavily criticized for its essentialist conception of women, failing to account for differences in class and race, among other things. In their attempt to unveil a recognizable—we might even say universal—tradition of female literary creation, Gilbert and Gubar occasionally sacrifice attention to difference.

The particular gynocritical approach modelled by *Madwoman* locates the study firmly in the context of Anglo-American second-wave feminism and subscribes to a binary logic of male and female. French feminist theorists, meanwhile, were theorizing the concept of difference in an attempt to move beyond such an oppositional logic that simply reversed the hierarchy. Hélène Cixous,* for example, proposed so-called écriture féminine, which was less about who (man or woman) had authored a text, and more about the ways in which anybody's writing could explode the oppositional binaries that structured patriarchal ideology.*

Gilbert and Gubar's strongly biographical approach has also been criticized as it limits texts to reflecting their authors' lives. To a certain extent, their readings can be seen to remain trapped in a patriarchal understanding of authorship, where only the figure of the author gives meaning to a literary text. Again, French theory of the period was working in a different direction. Roland Barthes'* influential essay "The Death of the Author" argues that author-based readings limit the potential meanings of complex texts.

Though *Madwoman* is now often considered "of its time," it is important to recognize its huge achievement of creating a context for feminist literary analysis. Apart from anything else, it is now itself a record of feminist history.

MODULE 8
PLACE IN THE AUTHOR'S WORK

KEY POINTS

- *The Madwoman in the Attic* was written early in Sandra M. Gilbert and Susan Gubar's careers, but nevertheless represents their overarching contribution to the field.
- Both Gilbert and Gubar stayed committed to feminist literary criticism throughout their careers, and this is reflected in their publications.
- *Madwoman* and its authors remain significant touchstones in feminist literary analysis.

Positioning

Sandra M. Gilbert and Susan Gubar had both just started in academia when they began working on *The Madwoman in the Attic: The Woman Writer and the Nineteenth-Century Literary Imagination*. The book is the culmination of, and in a certain sense maps, their own first encounter with women's writing as a distinct category, as well as their own feminist awakening. Although their engagement with the writers under consideration began accidentally—the necessity of teaching a module on women's writing—both authors devoted the majority of their subsequent careers to the collaborative analysis of women's literary tradition and poetics, for which the ideas took shape in this first book. Both Gilbert and Gubar went on to be the recipients of major fellowships and grants (such as Guggenheim and Rockefeller Fellowships) for related projects. This early work can hence be seen as formative for their respective careers, and their contribution to the field of women's literary scholarship has in turn been formative for the field.

> ❝ The book—or rather, the idea and plan for the book—seized us in a way that we felt was truly astonishing: we were taken out of ourselves, that is, transported out of our 'regular' academic and personal lives by a series of epiphanies that altered our thinking, our careers, and even our *selves* with what now seems like exceptional speed. ❞
>
> Sandra M. Gilbert, "Conversions of the Mind" in *Gilbert and Gubar's* The Madwoman in the Attic *after Thirty Years*

Gilbert and Gubar went on to produce both original scholarship in the form of their three-volume follow-up publication *No Man's Land: The Place of the Woman Writer in the Twentieth Century* (1988-1994), which extended their analysis of female poetics into the twentieth century, and did important work as anthologists, ensuring the ready availability of women's writing in English through the collation of their *Norton Anthology of Literature by Women: The Tradition in English* (1985).

Integration

Both Gilbert and Gubar forged careers as feminist literary historians. *Madwoman* remains, for both women, a defining academic achievement, though it is far from their only intervention. They expanded this first volume with a three-volume analysis of twentieth-century women's writing, though it focuses primarily on Modernist writers. In this substantial intervention, Gilbert and Gubar aimed to develop the argument they had made about nineteenth-century women's writing. If at the time they were writing the Victorian period was marked by a stable canon that was in need of rupturing, the instability of the early twentieth-century canon offered a contrasting field of inquiry. Here, the related but distinctive question is, how is women's writing affected by active canon formation? Gilbert and Gubar claim, "we are, we should stress, *de*scribing, not *pre*scribing, for our ultimate goal is to record and analyze the history that has made all of us who we are."[1]

They also did important work as the editors of *The Norton Anthology of Literature by Women: The Tradition in English* (1985), which made women's writing across history visible and readily available for study. Across all these projects, their commitment to a distinctive female literary history has remained constant. Even Gubar's more recent turn to life-writing* can be read in the vein of her longstanding feminism as a form of consciousness-raising.*

Significance

Madwoman made the names of Gilbert and Gubar, and indeed of Gilbert-and-Gubar,[2] and it remains, for both authors, their most well-known and oft-cited work. This is evidenced not least by the second, millennial edition Yale University Press published in 2000. *Madwoman* has significantly influenced literary feminism as well as feminist history. The prevalence of personal narratives of intellectual discovery, coupled with strong emotions of joy as evidenced, for example, in the thirtieth anniversary volume, are testament to *Madwoman's* enduring legacy and effect on new generations of feminist literary scholars.

While *Madwoman's* undeniably euro-centric, colour- and class-blind approach as well its straightforward reliance on author biographies have been heavily critiqued, Gilbert and Gubar's reputation as founding mothers of feminist literary scholarship is undisputed. *Madwoman* "contributed both courage and tools to that visionary period."[3] Both the courage and the tools remain vital to contemporary political projects that agitate for equality in the realm of cultural production and representation.

NOTES

1   Sandra M. Gilbert and Susan Gubar, *No-Man's Land: The Place of the Woman Writer in the Twentieth Century*, vol. 1, (New Haven, CT: Yale University Press, 1988), ·—•

2   Sandra M. Gilbert and Susan Gubar, *The Madwoman in the Attic: The Woman Writer and the Nineteenth-Century Literary Imagination*, 2nd ed. (New Haven, CT: Yale University Press, 2000), ··•

3   Annette R. Federico, "'Bursting All the Doors': *The Madwoman in the Attic* after Thirty Years," in *Gilbert and Gubar's* The Madwoman in the Attic *after Thirty Years*, ed. by Annette R. Federico (Columbia: University of Missouri Press, 2009), 23.

SECTION 3
IMPACT

MODULE 9
THE FIRST RESPONSES

KEY POINTS

- *The Madwoman in the Attic* was met with great interest upon initial publication and was widely reviewed as a ground-breaking piece of feminist criticism.

- One of the key critiques of *Madwoman* concerned the book's tendency to universalize women's experience across differences in nationality, class, race, and sexuality.

- Gilbert and Gubar have staunchly defended their approach, despite subsequent critiques.

Criticism

The Madwoman in the Attic: The Woman Writer and the Nineteenth-Century Literary Imagination was met with an overwhelming response upon first publication, widely reviewed both in academic journals and in the wider press—remarkable for an academic volume. Early academic reviews declared *Madwoman* "nothing short of breathtaking"[1] and "a jubilant achievement"[2] and included prescient predictions of its field-defining status: "It is the work to which most feminist criticism and theory these next years will have to refer, in support and disagreement."[3] More mainstream publications, too, issued gushing reviews of Sandra M. Gilbert and Susan Gubar's hefty tome, with one reviewer exclaiming: "I read it in a state of sustained excitement because it offered a new way of seeing,"[4] and the *New York Times* recommended it as summer reading the following year.[5] It was also shortlisted for the Pulitzer Prize, an unprecedented event for a work of academic scholarship at the time. The feminist exhilaration, which for Gilbert

> ** ** *The Madwoman in the Attic* is less a revolutionary manifesto than a bible of revolution, giving definitive form to the collective work of a decade. ** **
>
> Nina Auerbach, "Review of *The Madwoman in the Attic*"

and Gubar was such an important part of writing *Madwoman*, seems to have transferred itself to its early readers.

From the beginning, reservations were also expressed across the academic and mainstream media. These primarily concerned Gilbert and Gubar's positing of a universal feminine experience and, connected to this, their use of historical evidence. Fellow literary scholar Nina Auerbach,* for instance, "feared the reconstruction of a corporate womanhood as undifferentiated as the angels and monsters Gilbert/Gubar began by wanting to slay."[6] Rosemary Dinnage* accused Gilbert and Gubar of historical anachronism because they read nineteenth-century literature through a twentieth-century feminist lens which, for example, leads to a misreading of the idea of maternity as horrifying in women's understanding of their selves.[7]

Authors' Response

Gilbert and Gubar themselves did not immediately respond to this criticism, though both address these and subsequent points of critique much later, for example in their introduction to the second edition of *Madwoman* (2000). However, the book did initiate a debate amongst scholars right from the start, clearly tapping into a ready audience for feminist critique and in particular feminist revision—in this case of received historical narratives and narratives of the literary tradition. One arena for this debate was the letters section of *The New York Review of Books*, where Nina Auerbach and Sandra Zagarell* published a response to Rosemary Dinnage's review of *Madwoman* in that same publication. Auerbach and Zagarell take Dinnage, whose review had been mixed, to task for "a biased presentation of a learned and scrupulous work of scholarship."[8] Given Auerbach's own reservations about Gilbert and Gubar's book, particularly its "sometimes shaky methods,"[9] this strong defense may seem surprising. But it prefigures what has become a common critical position on the work, emphasizing its political importance and courage over its conceptual and methodological limitations. This stance is encapsulated in Zagarell and Auerbach's judgment of *Madwoman* as "a complex and important work of feminist literary criticism."[10] Dinnage's reply is also printed, which clearly shows the editors of *The New York Review of Books*, a commercial publication, deemed the debate relevant to the general public.

Conflict And Consensus

While the debate has continued across the decades, Gilbert and Gubar did not revise their position in light of this early criticism. On the contrary, they continued their critical project with the three-volume follow-up study of Modernist writing, *No-Man's Land* (1988-94). Their approach was again historical and aimed at revising the canon through reassessing literary history and narratives of literary tradition. In their preface to the first volume, they explain, "we are, we should stress, *de*scribing, not *pre*scribing, for our ultimate goal is to record and analyze the history that has made all of us who we are."[11] More recently they have firmly remarked, "We don't repudiate anything. Not at all. It had to be done."[12]

Subsequent debate, and with it the particular critiques of *Madwoman*, moved on from second-wave feminism to the poststructuralist* feminist inquiries of the 1980s and 1990s. With their politically motivated focus on difference, emerging black* and lesbian feminisms* strongly objected to *Madwoman's* tendencies toward sweeping generalizations about women writers as these seemed to imply white, middle-class, and heterosexual subjects only.

NOTES

1   Annette Kolodny, "Review of *The Madwoman in the Attic*," *American Literature* 52.1 (1980): 129.

2   Nina Auerbach, "Review of *The Madwoman in the Attic*," *Victorian Studies* 23.4 (1980): 507.

3   Helene Moglen, "Review of *The Madwoman in the Attic*," *Nineteenth-Century Literature* 35.2 (1980): 229.

4   Frances Taliaferro, "Review of *The Madwoman in the Attic*," *Harper's* (December 1979): 23.

5   Marlene Tromp, "Modeling the *Madwoman*: Feminist Movements and the Academy," in *Gilbert and Gubar's* The Madwoman in the Attic *after Thirty Years*, ed. by Annette R. Federico (Columbia: University of Missouri Press, 2009), 41.

6   Auerbach, "Review," 506.

7   Rosemary Dinnage, "Re-creating Eve," *The New York Review of Books*, 20 December 1979: 6-8.

8   Sandra Zagarell and Nina Auerbach, "Men, Women, and Lit.," *The New York Review of Books*, 6 March 1980, http://www.nybooks.com/articles/1980/03/06/men-women-and-lit/

9   Auerbach, "Review," 506.

10 Zagarell and Auerbach, "Men."

11 Sandra M. Gilbert and Susan Gubar, "Introduction," in *No-Man's Land: The Place of the Woman Writer in the Twentieth Century*, (New Haven: Yale University Press, 1988), 1: ---••

12 Annette R. Federico, "'Bursting All the Doors': *The Madwoman in the Attic* after Thirty Years," in *Gilbert and Gubar's* The Madwoman in the Attic *after Thirty Years*, ed. by Annette R. Federico (Columbia: University of Missouri Press, 2009), 11.

MODULE 10
THE EVOLVING DEBATE

KEY POINTS

- Important critiques were levied against *The Madwoman in the Attic* throughout the 1980s and 1990s, including from a postcolonial perspective.
- *Madwoman* became representative of so-called gynocriticism.
- *Madwoman*'s enduring impact can be seen in the subsequent projects of literary recovery it has enabled.

Uses And Problems

The poststructuralist critiques of *The Madwoman in the Attic: The Woman Writer and the Nineteenth-Century Literary Imagination* continued throughout the 1980s and 1990s as the field of feminist literary theory became more established within academia, and feminist discourse and activism in popular culture became more familiar. An increased focus on differences between women challenged unquestioned assumptions of women's solidarity. Toril Moi,* for instance, critiqued *Madwoman*'s methodology: "The concern with wholeness, with the woman writer as the *meaning* of the texts studies, is here pressed to its logical conclusion: the desire to write the narrative of a mighty 'Ur-woman'."[1] Moi argues that Sandra M. Gilbert and Susan Gubar remain entrenched in a patriarchal literary approach. Rather than fighting to have women accepted as authorities on par with men, the entire idea of authority should be questioned.

This is most notably enacted in Gayatri Chakravarty Spivak's* critique of Gilbert and Gubar's reading of Bertha Mason in *Jane Eyre*. Spivak offers a postcolonial, anti-imperialist reading of Bertha,

> **❝**It is hard to exaggerate the enormity of the task these critics set themselves. In retrospect, we can see the undertaking as foolhardy, the impossible scope of these works inevitably opening the authors to critiques from every side, but it was also brave and audacious.**❞**
>
> Mary Eagleton, "Literary Representations of Women," in *A History of Feminist Literary Criticism*

pitched against Gilbert and Gubar's reading of Rochester's first wife as Jane's double. For Spivak, that is a reductive reading, denying Bertha her own individuality and humanity as a racially "other" subject. In this way, Gilbert and Gubar's interpretation of the novel fails to account for "the unquestioned ideology of imperialist axiomatics" and reproduces the "epistemic violence of imperialism."[2]

Gilbert and Gubar continued their project unabatedly while also regularly responding to the charges of sexism and racism that were brought against them.[3] In the preface to the second edition of *Madwoman*, for example, they declare, "But such nuance may be precisely what we couldn't afford at a time when it was enough suddenly to see that there could be a new way of seeing."[4]

Despite the heated debate, *Madwoman* remained an influential text—it turned into an inevitable reference point, even for diverging arguments which further enshrined the volume in the canon of feminist literary criticism. *Madwoman*'s significance to the field, methodologically and in terms of content, is evidenced by its resilience in the face of rereading as it becomes itself the object of feminist revision and critiques of canon formation.

Schools Of Thought

Madwoman was foundational for the field of feminist literary theory as well as for feminist literary history. In particular, it was key to the formation of Anglo-American feminist theory, which focused on representations of women and texts written by women. It is often categorized as an example of what Showalter called gynocriticism. Gynocriticisim replaces earlier revisionary readings of representations of women, such as were offered by Kate Millet, with "the study of women as writers, and its subjects are the history, styles, themes, genres, and structures of writing by women; the psychodynamics of female creativity; the trajectory of the individual or collective female career; and the evolution and laws of a female literary tradition."[5] It sounds like a description of *Madwoman*, and although Showalter takes Gilbert and Gubar to task for inadvertently reproducing patriarchal narratives of women's inferiority and is troubled by the implication of female deceitfulness that follows from Gilbert and Gubar's narrative of "submerged" rebellion, she lists *Madwoman* as a foundational text of gynocriticism.

While feminist theory has since expanded to focus on difference as well as similarity, the project of historical revision and canon formation continues.

In Current Scholarship
As evidenced by the 2009 publication of a collection of essays dedicated to the enduring influence of *Madwoman* in current scholarship, Gilbert and Gubar's project continues to resonate. The volume shows how the mode of close reading modelled by Gilbert and Gubar as well as their contribution to canon formation still elicit responses today, ranging from studies of seventeenth-century English poet John Milton to eco-criticism* to trauma theory.*

Madwoman is frequently posited as an inspirational text by scholars who share a commitment to the sustained analysis of the effects of gender on lives and texts.[6] The work of recovering women's literary history and tradition is ongoing, with projects including large-scale endeavours such as Palgrave Macmillan's ongoing multi-volume *The*

History of British Women's Writing and its recently launched Contemporary Women's Writing series. The forthcoming Edinburgh *Companion to Experimental Writing by Women* responds to an earlier publication, *The Routledge Companion to Experimental Literature* (2012) which, while compendious in geographical and formal range, includes only one chapter dedicated to women's writing and for the most part takes men's texts for its case studies. An even more recent example is the *Cambridge Companion to Irish Poets* (2017), which includes only four women poets (and 26 men), as well as only four women contributors. This has led to a declared boycott of gender-imbalanced anthologies and conferences by Irish women poets. There is also more isolated recuperative work, for example the Dorothy Richardson Scholarly Editions Project.

NOTES

1   Toril Moi, *Sexual/Textual Politics: Feminist Literary Theory* (London: Routledge, 2003), 66.

2   Gayatri Chakravorty Spivak, "Three Women's Texts and a Critique of Imperialism," *Critical Inquiry* 12.1 (1985): 248; 254.

3   See Susan Gubar, "What Ails Feminist Criticism?" *Critical Inquiry* 24.4 (1998): 878-902.

4   Sandra M. Gilbert and Susan Gubar, *The Madwoman in the Attic: The Woman Writer and the Nineteenth-Century Literary Imagination*, 2nd ed. (New Haven, CT: Yale University Press, 2000), ···.

5   Elaine Showalter, "Feminist Criticism in the Wilderness," *Critical Inquiry* 8.2 (1981): 184-5.

6   See Marlene Tromp, "Modeling the *Madwoman*: Feminist Movements and the Academy," in *Gilbert and Gubar's* The Madwoman in the Attic *after Thirty Years*, ed. by Annette R. Federico (Columbia: University of Missouri Press, 2009), 34-59.

MODULE 11
IMPACT AND INFLUENCE TODAY

KEY POINTS

- In current scholarship, *The Madwoman in the Attic* is still often positioned as a pioneering and inspirational text that initiates feminist awakenings.
- Despite appearances, *Madwoman* has common interests with postcolonial and queer theory.
- Recent feminist work is challenging some of the critical narratives that have solidified around *Madwoman*.

Position

The Madwoman in the Attic: The Woman Writer and the Nineteenth-Century Literary Imagination's relevance today is undiminished. It is seen as a pioneering text of feminist literary history and theory, knowledge of which can be a source of strength for contemporary feminists because it inscribes a tradition of feminist production and of feminist practice. It is often positioned as a text that initiates a feminist awakening, especially for second-wave feminists,[1] but also remains "controversial and intoxicating" for present-day students.[2] Its relevance to the field is manifest in the dedicated publications celebrating *Madwoman*'s anniversaries.

As debates around canon formation, women's struggle in a patriarchal cultural and political system, and modes of resistance continue, *Madwoman* is frequently re-positioned, but always remains an indispensable touchstone. To use Elaine Showalter's words, it has been one of a handful of truly "transformative" works of criticism[3] and a precursor to ongoing work in feminist revision and recovery.

> ❝ [A]s the first in a series, [*Madwoman*] sets in motion a train of feminist thought that can then be followed up to our present day. ❞
>
> Susan Fraiman, "After Gilbert and Gubar: Madwomen Inspired by *Madwoman*," in *Gilbert and Gubar's* The Madwoman in the Attic *after Thirty Years*

Interaction

Madwoman's ongoing relevance can be seen in the number of publications and approaches that take it as their starting point, even if that starting point is one of departure. Although criticized for its essentialist notion of women (by, for example, Gayatri Spivak and Toril Moi), and although this has been repeatedly defended by Gilbert and Gubar,[4] *Madwoman* shares with queer theory an interest in deviancy and "[i]ts method of skeptical close reading runs parallel to that of deconstruction."[5] It can be seen as interacting in multiple ways with the critiques waged over its argument and method, even beyond the claim to historically representative value. Showalter's positioning of *Madwoman* alongside key texts of queer theory—Eve Kosofsky Sedgwick's *Between Men*—and postcolonial theory— Edward Said's *Orientalism*—also speaks to the volume's potential for connection across these different discourses rather than the more familiar narrative of rupture. *Madwoman*, with its unmistakable tone of excitement and its unabashed inclusion of personal anecdote— for instance when Gubar relates the anecdote of reading Gilbert's Emily Dickinson paper at a conference while preoccupied by "the tingling as milk soaked the front of the only dress I possessed that would cover my then […] ample breasts"[6]—can also be read as an early example of the type of writing that has become more prominent with the advent of affect theory* (see also Module 12).

The Continuing Debate

As feminist inquiry has become more firmly established within the academy, the ways in which it tells its own history has begun to be questioned. Clare Hemmings'* work in particular challenges the dominant metaphor of waves (e.g. second-wave feminism) and the narratives of rupture these convey. At the same time, she challenges straightforward progress narratives of feminist achievement. Instead, she contends, different aspects of feminist theory and activism coincide across time, especially once the geographical scope of feminisms under consideration is widened. Hemmings reminds us that it is important to reflect on the stories we tell of ourselves as feminists and to pay particular attention to whom we cite when we narrate a history of feminist theory, but we can also extend this to include women's writing. Hemmings calls this "citation tactics,"[7] and this is the point where, perhaps surprisingly, her work intersects with Gilbert and Gubar's revisionary project that interceded in literary canon formation by citing different texts.

More recent feminist work has turned towards a global context, diversifying the concept of "woman" and recovering feminist narratives from other cultural contexts. Similarly, recent debates around transgender women challenge ideas of womanhood espoused for example in *Madwoman* and force feminists to persistently reassess—re-vise—their position.

NOTES

1 See Tromp's survey of 400 academics regarding the role *Madwoman* had played in their own feminist and intellectual development (Tromp, "Modeling the *Madwoman*," 56).

2 Annette R. Federico, "Acknowledgements," in *Gilbert and Gubar's* The Madwoman in the Attic *after Thirty Years*, ed. by Annette R. Federico (Columbia: University of Missouri Press, 2009), n. p.

3 Elaine Showalter, "Gilbert & Gubar's *The Madwoman in the Attic* After Thirty Years," *Victorian Studies* 53.4 (2011): 715.

4   See Susan Gubar, "What Ails Feminist Criticism?" *Critical Inquiry* 24:4
    (1998): 878-902.

5   Susan Fraiman, "After Gilbert and Gubar: Madwomen Inspired by
    Madwoman," in *Gilbert and Gubar's* The Madwoman in the Attic *after Thirty
    Years*, ed. by Annette R. Federico (Columbia: University of Missouri Press,
    2009), 33.

6   Sandra M. Gilbert and Susan Gubar, *The Madwoman in the Attic: The
    Woman Writer and the Nineteenth-Century Literary Imagination*, 2nd ed.
    (New Haven, CT: Yale University Press, 2000), p. ···.

7   Clare Hemmings, *Why Stories Matter: The Political Grammar of Feminist
    Theory* (Durham: Duke University Press, 2011), 20.

MODULE 12
WHERE NEXT?

KEY POINTS

- *The Madwoman in the Attic* is considered a classic of early feminist critique in literature and remains a critical touchstone for developing debates.

- One of the biggest conceptual challenges to contemporary woman-centered feminism is trans-feminism, which will test the inclusionary practice modelled by *Madwoman*.

- *Madwoman* is a seminal volume of literary analysis that marries feminist scholarship with feminist practice in unprecedented and still rarely reproduced ways.

Potential

The Madwoman in the Attic: The Woman Writer and the Nineteenth-Century Literary Imagination is already considered a classic, and its influence as such is likely to continue. It is one of the most frequently cited volumes of second-wave feminist literary criticism, and both of its authors remain vocal contributors to feminist debates today. *Madwoman* serves as an important point of reference that establishes a critic's credibility and authority in the field of literary feminism; it continues to stimulate debate, and even as new critical approaches enter the academy—e.g. ecocriticism, trauma theory—their proponents find themselves turning back to *Madwoman* for context and/or critical material.

As surveys by the non-profit feminist organization VIDA: Women in Literary Arts persuasively demonstrate, women remain underrepresented in the literary arts. In order to assess this representation, VIDA looks at the gender of both reviewers of books

> ❝ We were not surprised to find that men dominate the pages of venues that are known to further one's career. ❞
>
> VIDA: Women in Literary Arts

and the gender of authors reviewed in influential literary journals and periodicals such as the *London Review of Books* or the *New York Times Book Review.*[1] As the recent reconfiguration of the VIDA count, which first took place in 2010, demonstrates, even in 2010, diversity in feminist activism was not a given, and in 2014, an expanded survey that accounted for race and ethnicity was introduced. The survey showed the importance of intersectional feminist critique and activism, as BAME (Black, Asian, and minority ethnic) women writers and reviewers were significantly underrepresented. This demonstrates the ongoing need for the type of feminist inquiry married with self-reflective activism modelled by *Madwoman*.

Future Directions

Madwoman's legacies are plentiful and far-reaching, and the project of literary recovery they helped initiate is far from complete. Some of the ways in which their work is being continued and will remain influential include the prominence of life-writing in scholarly inquiry as well as new modes of writing that bring together creative and critical styles in an attempt to displace the convention of "objectivity" in scholarly inquiry. The Oxford Centre for Life-Writing at Wolfson College testifies to the institutional validation of the former, offering a forum for discussion as well as financial aid for projects exploring the form. Historically, it is a form associated with women's writing, and its institutionalization speaks to the sustained influence of feminist theory and activism. Modes of writing that bring together critical and creative practice can also be traced back to

Gilbert and Gubar's work in the way that they strive to disrupt conventional discourses and representations. Clare Hemmings's forthcoming study of the anarchist revolutionary Emma Goldman, for instance, includes her imaginative responses to gaps in Goldman's archive. Her aim is to explore the role affective attachments play in the histories we write.[2] This is reminiscent of Gilbert's anecdote of reading *Jane Eyre* together with her young daughter and this initiating her inquiry into women's writing as having a history and a poetics.

One of the biggest conceptual challenges to contemporary woman-centred feminism is trans-feminism, and this will test the inclusionary practice modelled by *Madwoman*.

Summary

With *Madwoman,* Gilbert and Gubar helped show the importance of literary representation to social and cultural change as well as to personal development. The history of its reception elucidates key moments and sticking points in feminist literary criticism and the ongoing project of writing women's literary history. It also shows the importance of debate and disagreement to political progress and the richness of Gilbert and Gubar's propositions, which sparked important poststructural and postcolonial contributions to feminist criticism and continue to reverberate today. *Madwoman*'s modelling of feminist practice—through its valuing of pedagogy, its resolutely collaborative approach, and its explicit narration of personal experience and how that could be linked back to a broader social experience—remain pertinent and unusual to this day. The need for feminist solidarity—solidarity that accounts for differences between women by coming together purposefully and strategically but never with complacency, especially when it comes to challenging cultural representations of women—is as vital in 2018 as it was in 1979. Campaigns such as #metoo take these forms of solidarity and critiques of the cultural representation of women into the age of new media. *Madwoman*

NOTES

1   VIDA: Women in the Literary Arts, accessed February 1, 2018, http://www.vidaweb.org

2   Clare Hemmings, *Considering Emma Goldman: Feminist Political Ambivalence and the Imaginative Archive* (Durham: Duke University Press, 2018).

GLOSSARY

GLOSSARY OF TERMS

Aesthetic: having to do with the perception and appreciation of beauty; relating to sensory perception.

Affect theory: a strand of critical theory that gained influence in the early 2000s and argues for the importance of bodies and sensations to analytical projects. Prominent theorists include Brian Massumi and Lauren Berlant.

Angel in the House: derived from Coventry Patmore's poem of the same title, the idea of the angel in the house suggested that women were naturally better suited to the quiet domestic life, primarily oriented towards dutifully caring for their husbands and children.

Black feminism: influenced by the civil rights movement, it stressed the specific experience of race as it intersects with gender. It developed in response to a perceived bias in the feminist* movement towards white women.

Canon/canonical: in the context of literature, a collection of works that have conventionally been seen as especially significant. There is no fixed or stable list of such works, despite some efforts to make one.

Close reading: a method within literary studies that aims to analyze texts at the level of form as well as content.

Consciousness-raising: seeking to increase people's awareness of a social or political issue, especially in the context of feminism.*

Corpus: a body or collection of works, whether by a particular author (e.g., George Eliot's* corpus), or in a certain field (the corpus of second-wave feminist* works).

Deconstruction: an influential literary theory that originated with French philosopher Jacques Derrida.* Its method unpicks binary or oppositional meanings and exposes underlying hierarchies.

Eco-criticism: an interdisciplinary approach that brings together the study of literature and that of the environment.

Essentialist: refers to a belief that things have fixed, absolute characteristics (essences) and that these can be identified and expressed by philosophers or scientists.

Feminism (n. **feminist**): a political movement that advocates and agitates for equal rights between the sexes it encompasses a broad array of approaches and agendas, including Black feminism* or lesbian feminism.* Feminism is often divided into waves, beginning with the suffragette movement in the early twentieth century.

Formalist (n. formalism): an approach in literary criticism that focuses on the structural and literary features of a text (for example syntax, metaphor, stanzas). New Criticism* is an example of a formalist approach.

Gynocriticism: literary criticism that focuses exclusively on writing by women. It aims to recover women's texts and to read them in a feminist* context.

Ideology: a system of ideas that either underpin unconsciously or are adopted consciously by a particular group or society, especially a class or social group.

Intersectional analysis: argues that issues of social justice and equality must be analysed as complex intersections of various aspects including gender, sexuality, class, race, and disability.

Lesbian feminism: developed in the 1970s out of dissatisfaction with women's liberation as too heterosexual and gay liberation as too male-centered.

Life-writing: a broad term that refers to the recording of personal experience and memory; it includes autobiography, diaries, journals, oral history, recorded memories, letters, and memoirs.

Misogyny: hatred of or prejudice against women.

Modernism: a broad term that refers to a range of literary and artistic movements arising as a response to the social conditions of modernity; typically, it is used to describe works of the early twentieth century that are innovative or experimental in form.

New Criticism: a movement in literary studies that was especially dominant in US-American universities during the 1940s and 1950s and still has a marked effect on the discipline. It prioritized close reading of particular texts and tended to diminish the significance of context.

Oedipus complex: a psychoanalytic* theory established by Sigmund Freud* which proposes that, during a certain phase of their early development, children form an unconscious desire for their parent of the opposite sex.

Paranoid reading: a term coined by Eve Kosofsky Sedgwick, it draws on psychoanalytic* theory and describes a mode of reading that seeks to uncover concealed dynamics in texts (such as same-sex desire, homophobia, misogyny,* and utopianism).

Patriarchal: a term that describes societies, cultures, or institutions in which positions of authority tend to be occupied by men and in which values that favor men, or tend to reduce women to subsidiary positions, are dominant.

Phallic: pertaining to the phallus, which is understood to symbolize masculine or patriarchal authority.

Poetics: a branch of literary scholarship that deals especially with the forms and techniques of poetry; more broadly, the creative principles that underpin a literary, social, or cultural construction.

Poststructuralism: a school of critical thought that became especially influential from the 1980s. It consists of many different approaches, but they all share a skepticism towards language and meaning as straightforwardly knowable.

Psychoanalytical: relating to psychoanalysis, a set of therapeutic methods based on the discoveries and analyses of Sigmund Freud* and focusing on the relationship between conscious and unconscious elements in the patient's mind.

Romantic period/Romanticism: roughly, a period spanning the late eighteenth and early nineteenth centuries during which Romanticism was the dominant literary, artistic, and philosophical movement. Romanticism was characterized by an intense focus on sentiment, the emotions, and the individual.

Second-wave feminism: a phase in the development of feminist*
thought that expanded the focus of its analysis and demands for
equality to cover every area of women's experience, including
sexuality, family, and work. It follows from first-wave feminism, which
focused on political suffrage. Second-wave feminism in turn was
succeeded by third-wave feminism, which interrogated the idea of
"woman."

The personal is political: a slogan of second-wave feminism* that
insists that seemingly private matters (sexuality, family, work, domestic
life) are in fact sites for political struggle.

Transatlantic: typically refers to Britain and the United States,
though it refers more broadly and literally to countries on either side
of the Atlantic and the relationships between them.

Trauma theory: in literary studies, it refers to the tension between a
text and an unrepresentable event. An early influential text is Cathy
Caruth's *Unclaimed Experience* (1996).

 US-American: refers to the United States of America and
emphasizes the distinction between the United States and other parts
of the Americas.

US-American feminism: often distinguished from French
feminism,* its origins and impetus are associated with the 1960s civil
rights movement in the USA.

Victorian: relating to British history, culture, and literature during the
reign of Queen Victoria (1837–1901).

PEOPLE MENTIONED IN THE TEXT

Nina Auerbach (1943-2017) was a US-American literary scholar who was the John Welsh Centennial Professor of English Emerita at the University of Pennsylvania. Her most influential publications were in the fields of feminist theory and Victorian literature, including *Communities of Women* (1978).

Jane Austen (1775-1817) was an English novelist who became one of the most famous and significant writers of the nineteenth century. Her six major novels include *Sense and Sensibility* (1811), *Pride and Prejudice* (1813), and *Persuasion* (1818).

Elizabeth Barrett-Browning (1806-1861) was a nineteenth-century English poet born in the North East who became active in the literary scene of Victorian London, published widely, and was subsequently married to the poet Robert Browning. She is known for her sonnets and longer poems such as *Aurora Leigh* (1856).

Roland Barthes (1915-1980) was a French literary theorist who was an important contributor to post-structuralist thought. His major works include *Mythologies* (1972 [1957]) and *The Pleasure of the Text* (1975 [1973]).

Harold Bloom (b. 1930) is a US-American literary scholar and the Sterling Professor of the Humanities and English at Yale University, as well as the author of many books whose major themes have been influence, authority, and canonization.

Charlotte Brontë (1816–1855) was the eldest of the three Brontë sisters and a writer whose novels included *Jane Eyre* (1847), *Shirley* (1849), and *Villette* (1853).

Emily Brontë (1818–1848) was the middle sister of the three Brontës and a writer who produced one novel, *Wuthering Heights* (1847).

Kate Chopin (1850–1904) was a US-American writer who produced novels and short stories and whose key works include "A Pair of Silk Stockings" (1897) and *The Awakening* (1899).

Hélène Cixous (b. 1937) is a French feminist literary critic who is best known for her essay "The Laugh of the Medusa" (1975), which is seen as a founding text of French feminist theory. She was a founding member of the radical university at Vincennes, Paris.

Nancy F. Cott (b. 1945) is a US-American historian and the current Jonathan Trumbull Professor of American History at Harvard University. She is noted as a historian of sexuality and gender, with books such as *The Grounding of Modern Feminism* (1987) and *Public Vows: A History of Marriage and the Nation* (2000).

Jacques Derrida (1930–2004) was a French-Algerian philosopher whose writings on language and power became the foundations of Deconstruction,* a highly influential school of thought in late twentieth-century literary criticism. Key works include *Of Grammatology* (1976) and *Difference and Writing* (1978)

Emily Dickinson (1830–1886) was a US-American poet who produced a large corpus of poems, none of which were published during her lifetime but which gradually appeared in subsequent years and led to her being considered arguably one of the most important poets of the nineteenth century.

Rosemary Dinnage (1928-2015) was a British writer, psychologist, and public intellectual who contributed regularly to *The London Review of Books* and the *Times Literary Supplement*.

Ann Douglas (b. 1942) is a US-American scholar of literature and culture who was the first woman to teach in Princeton University's English Department. Her books include *The Feminization of American Culture* (1977) and *Terrible Honesty: Mongrel Manhattan in the 1920s* (1995).

George Eliot (1819-1880) is the pen name of Mary Ann Evans, a prominent English novelist of the nineteenth century born in the West Midlands. Her major novels include *Adam Bede* (1859), *Middlemarch* (1871-2), and *Daniel Deronda* (1876).

William Empson (1906-1984) was an English poet and critic who studied with I.A. Richards* in the 1920s and wrote the seminal *Seven Types of Ambiguity* (1930) based partly on the method of practical criticism that was practised in these classes.

Shulamith Firestone (1945-2012) was a North-American feminist activist who was a founding member of numerous radical feminist groups including the Redstockings. Her book *The Dialectic of Sex:The Case for a Feminist Revolution* (1970) was essential to second-wave feminism.

Sigmund Freud (1856-1939) was an Austrian neurologist and writer who founded the psychotherapeutic practice of psychoanalysis.

His establishment of concepts such as the unconscious, transference, and repression was extremely influential.

Betty Friedan (1921–2006) was a US-American feminist writer and activist who was a prominent figure in the women's liberation movement. Her book *The Feminine Mystique* (1963) was an early landmark of second-wave feminism.

Charlotte Perkins Gilman (1860–1935) was a US-American writer, activist and lecturer who produced work in a number of fields, including sociology, fiction, poetry, psychology, and feminism. She wrote widely, and her most famous work is "The Yellow Wallpaper" (1892).

Germaine Greer (b. 1939) is an Australian writer and activist whose debut publication, *The Female Eunuch* (1970) helped launch second-wave feminism. More recently, she has taken a controversial stance on transgender rights.

Clare Hemmings is a British feminist scholar and activist who is Professor of Feminist Theory at the London School of Economics. Her most influential publication is *Why Stories Matter* (2011).

D. H. Lawrence (1885–1930) was an English writer whose works included novels, short stories, essays, and poems. Born in the East Midlands, his work is both extremely influential and very controversial, especially for its sexual politics.

Gerda Lerner (1920–2013) was a US-American historian, born in Austria, whose prominent work includes *Black Women in White America: A Documentary History* (1972) and *The Creation of Patriarchy* (1986). She is a major figure in the development of women's history.

Norman Mailer (1923-2007) was a US-American author who wrote across genres and is best known for his engagement with the themes of fighting, sex, and masculinity. Among his significant works are *An American Dream* (1965), *The Executioner's Song* (1980), and *The Fight* (1975).

Henry Miller (1891-1980) was a US-American writer who was an expatriate in Paris and in Greece from 1930 to 1940. Informed by surrealism, his many works include *Tropic of Cancer* (1934), *Black Spring* (1936), *The Colossus of Maroussi* (1941), and *Big Sur and the Oranges of Hieronymus Bosch* (1957).

Kate Millet (1934-2017) was a US-American writer, artist, filmmaker, teacher, and activist who was one of the most prominent figures in the development of second-wave feminism and feminist cultural theory. Her first major book was *Sexual Politics* (1970).

Ellen Moers (1928-1978) was a US-American literary critic whose most prominent book was *Literary Women* (1976) and who also produced work on the figure of the dandy and on Theodore Dreiser. Her work was comparative in focus, as well as being informed by (and informing) second-wave feminism.

Toril Moi (b. 1953) is a Norwegian feminist* literary scholar who is currently Professor of English, Philosophy, and Theatre Studies at Duke University. Her 1986 study of second-wave feminism,* *Sexual/Textual Politics*, made a significant contribution to the field with its systematic comparison of Anglo-American and French feminist theories.

I. A. Richards (1893-1979) was an English literary critic, teacher, and scholar of language whose most significant contribution to the development of literary studies was the practice of Practical Criticism, a foundation for the method of close reading.

Christina Rossetti (1830–1894) was a nineteenth-century English poet who was a major figure in the Victorian literary sphere and whose works include the collection *Goblin Market and Other Poems* (1862), and *A Pageant and Other Poems* (1881).

Alice S. Rossi (1922–2009) was a US-American sociologist and feminist scholar who was Harriet Martineau professor of sociology at the University of Massachusetts and a founding member of the National Organization for Women. Her books include *Seasons of a Woman's Life* (1983) and *Of Human Bonding* (1990).

Edward Said (1935–2003) was an academic and public intellectual who was Professor of English and Comparative Literature at Columbia University and authored 18 books, among which the most prominent was *Orientalism* (1978). He was one of the key figures in the development of postcolonial studies.

Eve Kosofsky Sedgwick (1950–2009) was a writer, teacher, and activist who was one of the key figures in the development of queer theory and who had a significant impact on subsequent literary and cultural studies. Her major works include *Between Men* (1985), *Epistemology of the Closet* (1990), and *Tendencies* (1993).

Mary Wollstonecraft Shelley (1797–1851) was an English writer of fiction and non-fiction, best known for *Frankenstein: or, The Modern Prometheus* (1818), but also for novels such as *Perkin Warbeck* (1830) and the travel book *Rambles in Germany and Italy* (1844).

Elaine Showalter (b. 1941) is a US-American literary scholar who coined the term "gynocriticism" and has been a major figure in the development of feminist literary and cultural criticism. Her key works include *Toward a Feminist Poetics* (1979) and *The Female Malady* (1985).

Carroll Smith-Rosenberg (b. 1936) is a US-American scholar who is an Emerita Professor of History, American Culture, and Women's Studies at the University of Michigan. She has been a prominent historian of gender, sexuality, and Atlantic colonialism.

Patricia Meyers Spacks (b. 1929) is the Edgar F. Shannon Professor of Emerita in English at the University of Virginia, whose most recent publication is *On Rereading* (2011).

Gayatri Chakravorty Spivak (b. 1942) is an Indian feminist critic with a focus on postcolonial theory and a professor of English Literature at Columbia University. An influential proponent of deconstructionism, Spivak translated Derrida's *Of Grammatology*. Her key works include the essay "Can the Subaltern Speak?"

Gertrude Stein (1874–1946) was a US-American writer whose work is counted among the most significant of literary modernism. She lived in Paris from 1903, was an art collector and patron, and produced linguistically innovative texts including *Tender Buttons* (1912).

Marlene Tromp (b. 1966) is a US-American academic with a specialization in Victorian literature and culture who has published widely in the field, with a focus on gender and sexuality. She is professor of English and gender and women's studies at Arizona State University, as well as campus provost and executive vice chancellor at UC Santa Cruz.

77

Martha Vicinus (b. 1939) is a prominent literary scholar whose work has focused on class, gender, work, and sexuality. Her books include *The Industrial Muse* (1974), *A Widening Sphere: Changing Roles of Victorian Women* (1977), and *Independent Women: Work and Community for Single Women, 1850-1920* (1985).

Sandra Zagarell is the Donald R. Longman Professor of English at Oberlin College with a focus on nineteenth-century writing. She is a senior editor for the *Heath Anthology of American Literature*.

WORKS CITED

WORKS CITED

Auerbach, Nina. "Review of *The Madwoman in the Attic*," *Victorian Studies* 23.4 (1980): 505-7.

Brogan, Jacqueline V. "Interview with Sandra M. Gilbert," *Women's Studies* 38.4 (2009): 399-428.

Cain, William, ed. *Making Feminist History: The Literary Scholarship of Sandra M. Gilbert and Susan Gubar.* New York: Garland, 1993.

Demoor, Marysa and Katrien Heene. "State of the Art: Of Influences and Anxieties, Sandra Gilbert's Feminist Commitment," *The European Journal of Women's Studies* 9.2 (2002): 181-98.

Dinnage, Rosemary. "Re-creating Eve." *The New York Review of Books,* December 20, 1979, 6-8.

Eagleton, Mary. "Literary Representations of Women." In *A History of Feminist Literary Criticism*, edited by Gill Plain and Susan Sellers, 105-19. Cambridge: Cambridge University Press, 2007.

Federico, Annette R. "'Bursting All the Doors': *The Madwoman in the Attic* after Thirty Years." In *Gilbert and Gubar's* The Madwoman in the Attic *after Thirty Years*, edited by Annette R. Federico, 1-26. Columbia: University of Missouri Press, 2009.

Fraiman, Susan. "After Gilbert and Gubar: Madwomen Inspired by *Madwoman*." In *Gilbert and Gubar's* The Madwoman in the Attic *after Thirty Years*, edited by Annette R. Federico, 27-33. Columbia: University of Missouri Press, 2009.

Gilbert, Sandra M. "Conversions of the Mind." In *Gilbert and Gubar's* The Madwoman in the Attic *after Thirty Years*, edited by Annette R. Federico, ix-xiii. Columbia: University of Missouri Press, 2009.

Gilbert, Sandra M. and Susan Gubar. Introduction to *No-Man's Land: The Place of the Woman Writer in the Twentieth Century.* Vol 1, p. xi-xx. New Haven: Yale University Press, 1988.

Gilbert, Sandra M. and Susan Gubar. Interview by Eli Nadeau. *American Vanguard*, January 21, 2013. Accessed January 14, 2018. http://nbcc. americanvanguardpress.com/balakian–sandrof-awards/#topic_0

Gubar, Susan. "What Ails Feminist Criticism?" *Critical Inquiry* 24.4 (1998): 878-902.

Hemmings, Clare. *Why Stories Matter: The Political Grammar of Feminist Theory.* Durham: Duke University Press, 2011.

Hemmings, Clare. *Considering Emma Goldman: Feminist Political Ambivalence and the Imaginative Archive.* Durham: Duke University Press, 2018.

Kolodny, Annette. "Review of *The Madwoman in the Attic.*" *American Literature* 52.1 (1980): 128-32.

Moglen, Helene. "Review of *The Madwoman in the Attic.*" *Nineteenth-Century Literature* 35.2 (1980): 225-9.

Moi, Toril. *Sexual/Textual Politics: Feminist Literary Theory.* London: Routledge, 2003.

Showalter, Elaine. "Feminist Criticism in the Wilderness." *Critical Inquiry* 8.2 (1981): 179-205.

Showalter, Elaine. "Gilbert & Gubar's *The Madwoman in the Attic* After Thirty Years." *Victorian Studies* 53.4 (2011): 715-17.

Spivak, Gayatri Chakravorty. "Three Women's Texts and a Critique of Imperialism." *Critical Inquiry* 12.1 (1985): 243-61.

Taliaferro, Frances. "Review of *The Madwoman in the Attic.*" *Harper's,* December 1979, 23.

Tromp, Marlene. "Modeling the *Madwoman*: Feminist Movements and the Academy." In *Gilbert and Gubar's* The Madwoman in the Attic *after Thirty Years*, edited by Annette R. Federico, 34-59. Columbia: University of Missouri Press, 2009.

VIDA: Women in the Literary Arts. Accessed February 1, 2018. http://www.vidaweb.org

Zagarell, Sandra and Nina Auerbach. "Men, Women, and Lit." *The New York Review of Books,* March 6, 1980. Accessed February 1, 2018. http://www.nybooks.com/articles/1980/03/06/men-women-and-lit/.

THE MACAT LIBRARY
BY DISCIPLINE

AFRICANA STUDIES

Chinua Achebe's *An Image of Africa: Racism in Conrad's Heart of Darkness*
W. E. B. Du Bois's *The Souls of Black Folk*
Zora Neale Huston's *Characteristics of Negro Expression*
Martin Luther King Jr's *Why We Can't Wait*
Toni Morrison's *Playing in the Dark: Whiteness in the American Literary Imagination*

ANTHROPOLOGY

Arjun Appadurai's *Modernity at Large: Cultural Dimensions of Globalisation*
Philippe Ariès's *Centuries of Childhood*
Franz Boas's *Race, Language and Culture*
Kim Chan & Renée Mauborgne's *Blue Ocean Strategy*
Jared Diamond's *Guns, Germs & Steel: the Fate of Human Societies*
Jared Diamond's *Collapse: How Societies Choose to Fail or Survive*
E. E. Evans-Pritchard's *Witchcraft, Oracles and Magic Among the Azande*
James Ferguson's *The Anti-Politics Machine*
Clifford Geertz's *The Interpretation of Cultures*
David Graeber's *Debt: the First 5000 Years*
Karen Ho's *Liquidated: An Ethnography of Wall Street*
Geert Hofstede's *Culture's Consequences: Comparing Values, Behaviors, Institutes and Organizations across Nations*
Claude Lévi-Strauss's *Structural Anthropology*
Jay Macleod's *Ain't No Makin' It: Aspirations and Attainment in a Low-Income Neighborhood*
Saba Mahmood's *The Politics of Piety: The Islamic Revival and the Feminist Subject*
Marcel Mauss's *The Gift*

BUSINESS

Jean Lave & Etienne Wenger's *Situated Learning*
Theodore Levitt's *Marketing Myopia*
Burton G. Malkiel's *A Random Walk Down Wall Street*
Douglas McGregor's *The Human Side of Enterprise*
Michael Porter's *Competitive Strategy: Creating and Sustaining Superior Performance*
John Kotter's *Leading Change*
C. K. Prahalad & Gary Hamel's *The Core Competence of the Corporation*

CRIMINOLOGY

Michelle Alexander's *The New Jim Crow: Mass Incarceration in the Age of Colorblindness*
Michael R. Gottfredson & Travis Hirschi's *A General Theory of Crime*
Richard Herrnstein & Charles A. Murray's *The Bell Curve: Intelligence and Class Structure in American Life*
Elizabeth Loftus's *Eyewitness Testimony*
Jay Macleod's *Ain't No Makin' It: Aspirations and Attainment in a Low-Income Neighborhood*
Philip Zimbardo's *The Lucifer Effect*

ECONOMICS

Janet Abu-Lughod's *Before European Hegemony*
Ha-Joon Chang's *Kicking Away the Ladder*
David Brion Davis's *The Problem of Slavery in the Age of Revolution*
Milton Friedman's *The Role of Monetary Policy*
Milton Friedman's *Capitalism and Freedom*
David Graeber's *Debt: the First 5000 Years*
Friedrich Hayek's *The Road to Serfdom*
Karen Ho's *Liquidated: An Ethnography of Wall Street*

John Maynard Keynes's *The General Theory of Employment, Interest and Money*
Charles P. Kindleberger's *Manias, Panics and Crashes*
Robert Lucas's *Why Doesn't Capital Flow from Rich to Poor Countries?*
Burton G. Malkiel's *A Random Walk Down Wall Street*
Thomas Robert Malthus's *An Essay on the Principle of Population*
Karl Marx's *Capital*
Thomas Piketty's *Capital in the Twenty-First Century*
Amartya Sen's *Development as Freedom*
Adam Smith's *The Wealth of Nations*
Nassim Nicholas Taleb's *The Black Swan: The Impact of the Highly Improbable*
Amos Tversky's & Daniel Kahneman's *Judgment under Uncertainty: Heuristics and Biases*
Mahbub Ul Haq's *Reflections on Human Development*
Max Weber's *The Protestant Ethic and the Spirit of Capitalism*

FEMINISM AND GENDER STUDIES

Judith Butler's *Gender Trouble*
Simone De Beauvoir's *The Second Sex*
Michel Foucault's *History of Sexuality*
Betty Friedan's *The Feminine Mystique*
Saba Mahmood's *The Politics of Piety: The Islamic Revival and the Feminist Subject*
Joan Wallach Scott's *Gender and the Politics of History*
Mary Wollstonecraft's *A Vindication of the Rights of Woman*
Virginia Woolf's *A Room of One's Own*

GEOGRAPHY

The Brundtland Report's *Our Common Future*
Rachel Carson's *Silent Spring*
Charles Darwin's *On the Origin of Species*
James Ferguson's *The Anti-Politics Machine*
Jane Jacobs's *The Death and Life of Great American Cities*
James Lovelock's *Gaia: A New Look at Life on Earth*
Amartya Sen's *Development as Freedom*
Mathis Wackernagel & William Rees's *Our Ecological Footprint*

HISTORY

Janet Abu-Lughod's *Before European Hegemony*
Benedict Anderson's *Imagined Communities*
Bernard Bailyn's *The Ideological Origins of the American Revolution*
Hanna Batatu's *The Old Social Classes And The Revolutionary Movements Of Iraq*
Christopher Browning's *Ordinary Men: Reserve Police Batallion 101 and the Final Solution in Poland*
Edmund Burke's *Reflections on the Revolution in France*
William Cronon's *Nature's Metropolis: Chicago And The Great West*
Alfred W. Crosby's *The Columbian Exchange*
Hamid Dabashi's *Iran: A People Interrupted*
David Brion Davis's *The Problem of Slavery in the Age of Revolution*
Nathalie Zemon Davis's *The Return of Martin Guerre*
Jared Diamond's *Guns, Germs & Steel: the Fate of Human Societies*
Frank Dikotter's *Mao's Great Famine*
John W Dower's *War Without Mercy: Race And Power In The Pacific War*
W. E. B. Du Bois's *The Souls of Black Folk*
Richard J. Evans's *In Defence of History*
Lucien Febvre's *The Problem of Unbelief in the 16th Century*
Sheila Fitzpatrick's *Everyday Stalinism*

Eric Foner's *Reconstruction: America's Unfinished Revolution, 1863-1877*
Michel Foucault's *Discipline and Punish*
Michel Foucault's *History of Sexuality*
Francis Fukuyama's *The End of History and the Last Man*
John Lewis Gaddis's *We Now Know: Rethinking Cold War History*
Ernest Gellner's *Nations and Nationalism*
Eugene Genovese's *Roll, Jordan, Roll: The World the Slaves Made*
Carlo Ginzburg's *The Night Battles*
Daniel Goldhagen's *Hitler's Willing Executioners*
Jack Goldstone's *Revolution and Rebellion in the Early Modern World*
Antonio Gramsci's *The Prison Notebooks*
Alexander Hamilton, John Jay & James Madison's *The Federalist Papers*
Christopher Hill's *The World Turned Upside Down*
Carole Hillenbrand's *The Crusades: Islamic Perspectives*
Thomas Hobbes's *Leviathan*
Eric Hobsbawm's *The Age Of Revolution*
John A. Hobson's *Imperialism: A Study*
Albert Hourani's *History of the Arab Peoples*
Samuel P. Huntington's *The Clash of Civilizations and the Remaking of World Order*
C. L. R. James's *The Black Jacobins*
Tony Judt's *Postwar: A History of Europe Since 1945*
Ernst Kantorowicz's *The King's Two Bodies: A Study in Medieval Political Theology*
Paul Kennedy's *The Rise and Fall of the Great Powers*
Ian Kershaw's *The "Hitler Myth": Image and Reality in the Third Reich*
John Maynard Keynes's *The General Theory of Employment, Interest and Money*
Charles P. Kindleberger's *Manias, Panics and Crashes*
Martin Luther King Jr's *Why We Can't Wait*
Henry Kissinger's *World Order: Reflections on the Character of Nations and the Course of History*
Thomas Kuhn's *The Structure of Scientific Revolutions*
Georges Lefebvre's *The Coming of the French Revolution*
John Locke's *Two Treatises of Government*
Niccolò Machiavelli's *The Prince*
Thomas Robert Malthus's *An Essay on the Principle of Population*
Mahmood Mamdani's *Citizen and Subject: Contemporary Africa And The Legacy Of Late Colonialism*
Karl Marx's *Capital*
Stanley Milgram's *Obedience to Authority*
John Stuart Mill's *On Liberty*
Thomas Paine's *Common Sense*
Thomas Paine's *Rights of Man*
Geoffrey Parker's *Global Crisis: War, Climate Change and Catastrophe in the Seventeenth Century*
Jonathan Riley-Smith's *The First Crusade and the Idea of Crusading*
Jean-Jacques Rousseau's *The Social Contract*
Joan Wallach Scott's *Gender and the Politics of History*
Theda Skocpol's *States and Social Revolutions*
Adam Smith's *The Wealth of Nations*
Timothy Snyder's *Bloodlands: Europe Between Hitler and Stalin*
Sun Tzu's *The Art of War*
Keith Thomas's *Religion and the Decline of Magic*
Thucydides's *The History of the Peloponnesian War*
Frederick Jackson Turner's *The Significance of the Frontier in American History*
Odd Arne Westad's *The Global Cold War: Third World Interventions And The Making Of Our Times*

LITERATURE

Chinua Achebe's *An Image of Africa: Racism in Conrad's Heart of Darkness*
Roland Barthes's *Mythologies*
Homi K. Bhabha's *The Location of Culture*
Judith Butler's *Gender Trouble*
Simone De Beauvoir's *The Second Sex*
Ferdinand De Saussure's *Course in General Linguistics*
T. S. Eliot's *The Sacred Wood: Essays on Poetry and Criticism*
Zora Neale Huston's *Characteristics of Negro Expression*
Toni Morrison's *Playing in the Dark: Whiteness in the American Literary Imagination*
Edward Said's *Orientalism*
Gayatri Chakravorty Spivak's *Can the Subaltern Speak?*
Mary Wollstonecraft's *A Vindication of the Rights of Women*
Virginia Woolf's *A Room of One's Own*

PHILOSOPHY

Elizabeth Anscombe's *Modern Moral Philosophy*
Hannah Arendt's *The Human Condition*
Aristotle's *Metaphysics*
Aristotle's *Nicomachean Ethics*
Edmund Gettier's *Is Justified True Belief Knowledge?*
Georg Wilhelm Friedrich Hegel's *Phenomenology of Spirit*
David Hume's *Dialogues Concerning Natural Religion*
David Hume's *The Enquiry for Human Understanding*
Immanuel Kant's *Religion within the Boundaries of Mere Reason*
Immanuel Kant's *Critique of Pure Reason*
Søren Kierkegaard's *The Sickness Unto Death*
Søren Kierkegaard's *Fear and Trembling*
C. S. Lewis's *The Abolition of Man*
Alasdair MacIntyre's *After Virtue*
Marcus Aurelius's *Meditations*
Friedrich Nietzsche's *On the Genealogy of Morality*
Friedrich Nietzsche's *Beyond Good and Evil*
Plato's *Republic*
Plato's *Symposium*
Jean-Jacques Rousseau's *The Social Contract*
Gilbert Ryle's *The Concept of Mind*
Baruch Spinoza's *Ethics*
Sun Tzu's *The Art of War*
Ludwig Wittgenstein's *Philosophical Investigations*

POLITICS

Benedict Anderson's *Imagined Communities*
Aristotle's *Politics*
Bernard Bailyn's *The Ideological Origins of the American Revolution*
Edmund Burke's *Reflections on the Revolution in France*
John C. Calhoun's *A Disquisition on Government*
Ha-Joon Chang's *Kicking Away the Ladder*
Hamid Dabashi's *Iran: A People Interrupted*
Hamid Dabashi's *Theology of Discontent: The Ideological Foundation of the Islamic Revolution in Iran*
Robert Dahl's *Democracy and its Critics*
Robert Dahl's *Who Governs?*
David Brion Davis's *The Problem of Slavery in the Age of Revolution*

Alexis De Tocqueville's *Democracy in America*
James Ferguson's *The Anti-Politics Machine*
Frank Dikotter's *Mao's Great Famine*
Sheila Fitzpatrick's *Everyday Stalinism*
Eric Foner's *Reconstruction: America's Unfinished Revolution, 1863-1877*
Milton Friedman's *Capitalism and Freedom*
Francis Fukuyama's *The End of History and the Last Man*
John Lewis Gaddis's *We Now Know: Rethinking Cold War History*
Ernest Gellner's *Nations and Nationalism*
David Graeber's *Debt: the First 5000 Years*
Antonio Gramsci's *The Prison Notebooks*
Alexander Hamilton, John Jay & James Madison's *The Federalist Papers*
Friedrich Hayek's *The Road to Serfdom*
Christopher Hill's *The World Turned Upside Down*
Thomas Hobbes's *Leviathan*
John A. Hobson's *Imperialism: A Study*
Samuel P. Huntington's *The Clash of Civilizations and the Remaking of World Order*
Tony Judt's *Postwar: A History of Europe Since 1945*
David C. Kang's *China Rising: Peace, Power and Order in East Asia*
Paul Kennedy's *The Rise and Fall of Great Powers*
Robert Keohane's *After Hegemony*
Martin Luther King Jr.'s *Why We Can't Wait*
Henry Kissinger's *World Order: Reflections on the Character of Nations and the Course of History*
John Locke's *Two Treatises of Government*
Niccolò Machiavelli's *The Prince*
Thomas Robert Malthus's *An Essay on the Principle of Population*
Mahmood Mamdani's *Citizen and Subject: Contemporary Africa And The Legacy Of Late Colonialism*
Karl Marx's *Capital*
John Stuart Mill's *On Liberty*
John Stuart Mill's *Utilitarianism*
Hans Morgenthau's *Politics Among Nations*
Thomas Paine's *Common Sense*
Thomas Paine's *Rights of Man*
Thomas Piketty's *Capital in the Twenty-First Century*
Robert D. Putman's *Bowling Alone*
John Rawls's *Theory of Justice*
Jean-Jacques Rousseau's *The Social Contract*
Theda Skocpol's *States and Social Revolutions*
Adam Smith's *The Wealth of Nations*
Sun Tzu's *The Art of War*
Henry David Thoreau's *Civil Disobedience*
Thucydides's *The History of the Peloponnesian War*
Kenneth Waltz's *Theory of International Politics*
Max Weber's *Politics as a Vocation*
Odd Arne Westad's *The Global Cold War: Third World Interventions And The Making Of Our Times*

POSTCOLONIAL STUDIES

Roland Barthes's *Mythologies*
Frantz Fanon's *Black Skin, White Masks*
Homi K. Bhabha's *The Location of Culture*
Gustavo Gutiérrez's *A Theology of Liberation*
Edward Said's *Orientalism*
Gayatri Chakravorty Spivak's *Can the Subaltern Speak?*

PSYCHOLOGY

Gordon Allport's *The Nature of Prejudice*
Alan Baddeley & Graham Hitch's *Aggression: A Social Learning Analysis*
Albert Bandura's *Aggression: A Social Learning Analysis*
Leon Festinger's *A Theory of Cognitive Dissonance*
Sigmund Freud's *The Interpretation of Dreams*
Betty Friedan's *The Feminine Mystique*
Michael R. Gottfredson & Travis Hirschi's *A General Theory of Crime*
Eric Hoffer's *The True Believer: Thoughts on the Nature of Mass Movements*
William James's *Principles of Psychology*
Elizabeth Loftus's *Eyewitness Testimony*
A. H. Maslow's *A Theory of Human Motivation*
Stanley Milgram's *Obedience to Authority*
Steven Pinker's *The Better Angels of Our Nature*
Oliver Sacks's *The Man Who Mistook His Wife For a Hat*
Richard Thaler & Cass Sunstein's *Nudge: Improving Decisions About Health, Wealth and Happiness*
Amos Tversky's *Judgment under Uncertainty: Heuristics and Biases*
Philip Zimbardo's *The Lucifer Effect*

SCIENCE

Rachel Carson's *Silent Spring*
William Cronon's *Nature's Metropolis: Chicago And The Great West*
Alfred W. Crosby's *The Columbian Exchange*
Charles Darwin's *On the Origin of Species*
Richard Dawkin's *The Selfish Gene*
Thomas Kuhn's *The Structure of Scientific Revolutions*
Geoffrey Parker's *Global Crisis: War, Climate Change and Catastrophe in the Seventeenth Century*
Mathis Wackernagel & William Rees's *Our Ecological Footprint*

SOCIOLOGY

Michelle Alexander's *The New Jim Crow: Mass Incarceration in the Age of Colorblindness*
Gordon Allport's *The Nature of Prejudice*
Albert Bandura's *Aggression: A Social Learning Analysis*
Hanna Batatu's *The Old Social Classes And The Revolutionary Movements Of Iraq*
Ha-Joon Chang's *Kicking Away the Ladder*
W. E. B. Du Bois's *The Souls of Black Folk*
Émile Durkheim's *On Suicide*
Frantz Fanon's *Black Skin, White Masks*
Frantz Fanon's *The Wretched of the Earth*
Eric Foner's *Reconstruction: America's Unfinished Revolution, 1863-1877*
Eugene Genovese's *Roll, Jordan, Roll: The World the Slaves Made*
Jack Goldstone's *Revolution and Rebellion in the Early Modern World*
Antonio Gramsci's *The Prison Notebooks*
Richard Herrnstein & Charles A Murray's *The Bell Curve: Intelligence and Class Structure in American Life*
Eric Hoffer's *The True Believer: Thoughts on the Nature of Mass Movements*
Jane Jacobs's *The Death and Life of Great American Cities*
Robert Lucas's *Why Doesn't Capital Flow from Rich to Poor Countries?*
Jay Macleod's *Ain't No Makin' It: Aspirations and Attainment in a Low Income Neighborhood*
Elaine May's *Homeward Bound: American Families in the Cold War Era*
Douglas McGregor's *The Human Side of Enterprise*
C. Wright Mills's *The Sociological Imagination*

Thomas Piketty's *Capital in the Twenty-First Century*
Robert D. Putman's *Bowling Alone*
David Riesman's *The Lonely Crowd: A Study of the Changing American Character*
Edward Said's *Orientalism*
Joan Wallach Scott's *Gender and the Politics of History*
Theda Skocpol's *States and Social Revolutions*
Max Weber's *The Protestant Ethic and the Spirit of Capitalism*

THEOLOGY

Augustine's *Confessions*
Benedict's *Rule of St Benedict*
Gustavo Gutiérrez's *A Theology of Liberation*
Carole Hillenbrand's *The Crusades: Islamic Perspectives*
David Hume's *Dialogues Concerning Natural Religion*
Immanuel Kant's *Religion within the Boundaries of Mere Reason*
Ernst Kantorowicz's *The King's Two Bodies: A Study in Medieval Political Theology*
Søren Kierkegaard's *The Sickness Unto Death*
C. S. Lewis's *The Abolition of Man*
Saba Mahmood's *The Politics of Piety: The Islamic Revival and the Feminist Subject*
Baruch Spinoza's *Ethics*
Keith Thomas's *Religion and the Decline of Magic*

Macat Disciplines

*Access the greatest ideas and thinkers
across entire disciplines, including*

CRIMINOLOGY

Michelle Alexander's
*The New Jim Crow:
Mass Incarceration in the
Age of Colorblindness*

**Michael R. Gottfredson
& Travis Hirschi's**
A General Theory of Crime

Elizabeth Loftus's
Eyewitness Testimony

**Richard Herrnstein
& Charles A. Murray's**
*The Bell Curve: Intelligence and
Class Structure in American Life*

Jay Macleod's
*Ain't No Makin' It:
Aspirations and Attainment in a
Low-Income Neighborhood*

Philip Zimbardo's
The Lucifer Effect

Macat analyses are available from all good bookshops and libraries.

Access hundreds of analyses through one, multimedia tool.
Join free for one month **library.macat.com**

Macat Disciplines

Access the greatest ideas and thinkers across entire disciplines, including

Postcolonial Studies

Roland Barthes's *Mythologies*
Frantz Fanon's *Black Skin, White Masks*
Homi K. Bhabha's *The Location of Culture*
Gustavo Gutiérrez's *A Theology of Liberation*
Edward Said's *Orientalism*
Gayatri Chakravorty Spivak's *Can the Subaltern Speak?*

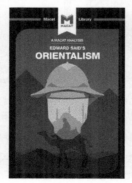

Macat Disciplines

Access the greatest ideas and thinkers across entire disciplines, including

GLOBALIZATION

Arjun Appadurai's, *Modernity at Large: Cultural Dimensions of Globalisation*

James Ferguson's, *The Anti-Politics Machine*

Geert Hofstede's, *Culture's Consequences*

Amartya Sen's, *Development as Freedom*

Macat analyses are available from all good bookshops and libraries.

Access hundreds of analyses through one, multimedia tool.
Join free for one month **library.macat.com**

Macat Disciplines

Access the greatest ideas and thinkers across entire disciplines, including

THE FUTURE OF DEMOCRACY

Robert A. Dahl's, *Democracy and Its Critics*
Robert A. Dahl's, *Who Governs?*
Alexis De Toqueville's, *Democracy in America*
Niccolò Machiavelli's, *The Prince*
John Stuart Mill's, *On Liberty*
Robert D. Putnam's, *Bowling Alone*
Jean-Jacques Rousseau's, *The Social Contract*
Henry David Thoreau's, *Civil Disobedience*

Macat analyses are available from all good bookshops and libraries.

Access hundreds of analyses through one, multimedia tool.
Join free for one month **library.macat.com**

Macat Pairs

Analyse historical and modern issues from opposite sides of an argument. Pairs include:

INTERNATIONAL RELATIONS IN THE 21ST CENTURY

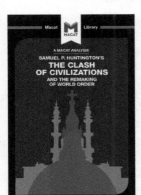

Samuel P. Huntington's
The Clash of Civilisations

In his highly influential 1996 book, Huntington offers a vision of a post-Cold War world in which conflict takes place not between competing ideologies but between cultures. The worst clash, he argues, will be between the Islamic world and the West: the West's arrogance and belief that its culture is a "gift" to the world will come into conflict with Islam's obstinacy and concern that its culture is under attack from a morally decadent "other."

Clash inspired much debate between different political schools of thought. But its greatest impact came in helping define American foreign policy in the wake of the 2001 terrorist attacks in New York and Washington.

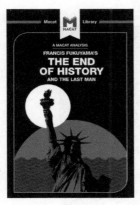

Francis Fukuyama's
The End of History and the Last Man

Published in 1992, *The End of History and the Last Man* argues that capitalist democracy is the final destination for all societies. Fukuyama believed democracy triumphed during the Cold War because it lacks the "fundamental contradictions" inherent in communism and satisfies our yearning for freedom and equality. Democracy therefore marks the endpoint in the evolution of ideology, and so the "end of history." There will still be "events," but no fundamental change in ideology.